SKINNY MEXICAN COOKING

SKINNY COOKING

Skinny Mexican

COOKING

◆———————◆

SUE SPITLER

SURREY BOOKS
CHICAGO

SKINNY MEXICAN COOKING is published by Surrey Books, Inc.
230 E. Ohio St., Suite 120, Chicago, IL 60611.

First edition: 1 2 3 4 5

This book is manufactured in the United States of America.

Library of Congress Cataloging-in-Publication data:

Spitler, Sue.
    Skinny Mexican cooking / by Sue Spitler.
    170p.   cm.
    Includes index.
    ISBN 0-940625-97-0 (pbk.)
    1. Reducing diets.   2. Cookery, Mexican.   I. Title.
RM222.2.S687 1996
641.5'63—dc20   95-41958
                                                               CIP

Editorial and production: *Bookcrafters, Inc., Chicago*
Art Director: *Joan Sommers Design, Chicago*
Cover and interior illustrations by *Mona Daly*

For free catalog and prices on quantity purchases, contact Surrey Books at the
address above.

This title is distributed to the trade by Publishers Group West.

Other titles in the "Skinny" Cookbooks Series:

Skinny Beef   *Skinny Pizzas*
Skinny Chicken   *Skinny Potatoes*
Skinny Chocolate   *Skinny Sandwiches*
Skinny Cookies, Cakes & Sweets   *Skinny Sauces & Marinades*
Skinny Grilling   *Skinny Seafood*
Skinny Italian Cooking   *Skinny Soups*
Skinny One-Pot Meals   *Skinny Spices*
Skinny Pasta   *Skinny Vegetarian Entrées*

To my many friends who love and enjoy Mexico
and its cuisine as much as I do!
Buen provecho!

Muchas gracias to Cindy Roth, a most enthusiastic associate in this South-of-the-Border cooking adventure; also to my good friend Jane Ellis for contributing her much appreciated cooking skills. Behind-the-scenes supporters included publisher Susan Schwartz, editor Gene DeRoin, and nutritionist Linda Yoakam, R.D.—heartfelt thanks to all.

CONTENTS

INTRODUCTION

Mexican food is as exciting, colorful, flavorful, and enjoyable as the country itself. Ingredients indigenous to this sub-tropical country provide inspiring flavors to stimulate weary palates and bring new excitement to the table. Mexican cuisine stems from a distinctive blending of Aztec, Mayan, and Spanish cultures, and it has been influenced over the years by people from many other countries. The cuisine has been adapted in the United States to create the many Tex-Mex and California-style dishes, such as fajitas and chimichangas, that are popular today. Mexican restaurants of every variety, offering authentic, family, or fast-food dining, have proliferated in this country and abroad. There's no doubt about it—everyone loves Mexican food!

But what about the nasty rumor that Mexican foods are high in fat and calories and less than healthful? Yes, Mexican recipes can be high in fat and calories. But in *Skinny Mexican Cooking,* a tempting variety of recipes, from appetizers through desserts, utilizes fat-reduced and fat-free ingredients and cooking methods to slim and trim dishes to healthy specifications. In accordance with the guidelines established by the American Heart Association, we made sure that none of the recipes exceeds 30 percent of calories from fat, and they all adhere to the following nutritional criteria:

TYPE OF RECIPE	MAXIMUM AMOUNTS PER SERVING		
	Calories	Cholesterol (mg)	Sodium (mg)
Appetizers	200	40	600
Beverages	200	50	600
Soups	200	50	600
Main-Dish Eggs	400	450	800
Main-Dish Meat, Poultry, Seafood	400	225	800
Main-Dish Meatless	500	120	800
One-Dish Meals	600	150	800
Salads	200	50	600
Vegetables	200	60	600
Sauces	100	25	600
Desserts	350	90	600

Specific nutritional information is provided for each recipe in this book, but please remember that nutritional data are not infallible. The nutritional analyses are derived using software highly regarded by nutritionists and dietitians, but they are meant to be used only as guidelines. Figures are based on actual laboratory values of ingredients, so results might vary slightly from those derived by using general rules of thumb, for example, "each fat gram contains 9 calories."

Ingredients noted as "optional," "to taste," or "garnish" are not included in nutritional analyses. When alternate choices or amounts of ingredients are given, the ingredient or amount listed first is used for analysis. Nutritional analyses also are based on the reduced-fat or fat-free cooking methods used in recipes; the addition of margarine, oil, or other ingredients to the recipes will invalidate data.

Other factors can also affect the accuracy of nutritional data, including the variability in sizes of fruits, vegetables, and other foods; variability in weights and measures of foods; and a possible plus or minus 20 percent error factor in the nutritional labeling of prepared foods.

If you have any health problems that require strict dietary requirements, it is important to consult a physician, dietitian, or nutritionist before using recipes in this or any other cookbook. Also, if you are a diabetic or require a diet that restricts calories, fat, or sodium, remember that the nutritional data may be accurate for the recipe as written but not for the food you cooked due to the variables explained above.

Until recent years, it was not easy to find the necessary ingredients to cook authentic Mexican food. Fortunately, ingredients such as fresh and dried chilies, tropical fruits, jicama, cactus, etc., are now readily available in local supermarkets, making the cuisine easily accessible to our own kitchens.

Skinny Mexican Cooking offers over 100 flavorful, healthful recipes for your enjoyment. You'll find them easy to make in little time and economical, too. With or without *mariachi* music, new food adventures await. So step South of the Border and enjoy your meal—*Buen provecho!*

INGREDIENTS

Fortunately, many of Mexico's wonderful chilies and other ingredients are now available in local stores. The listing that follows provides information for ingredients used in *Skinny Mexican Cooking* that you may not be familiar with.

Cactus The stems, or "paddles," of the nopal cactus are edible, tasting somewhat like green bell peppers. Select small to medium paddles that are firm and fresh looking. Before cooking, check that all the "stickers" have been removed; if not, cut or scrape them off. Cook the cactus as directed in the recipes; be sure to cook them until tender or they will exude a sticky substance similar to that of okra. Cactus can be refrigerated up to 2 weeks.

Chayote This is a type of squash that is also called vegetable pear or mirliton in this country. The squash has a pale green skin and whitish-green interior. It is crisp in texture, very subtle in flavor, and can be watery if overcooked. Select chayote that are firm and unblemished; store in the refrigerator up to 2 weeks.

Chilies, Dried Many varieties of dried peppers are available, packaged by specialty produce companies. Store dried chili peppers in airtight containers; if they become moist, they will mold and spoil. Like fresh peppers, the seeds and veins are quite hot, so discard them unless maximum hotness is desired. Sometimes the packaged chilies are soft and flexible, making them easy to work with; if hard and brittle, they can be softened by soaking in hot water or by heating briefly in a skillet.

Ancho Chili This chili is a dried poblano chili and is probably the most commonly used dried chili in Mexican cooking. It is a deep black-red color and wrinkled in appearance. Often used as a base for sauces or a seasoning for soups, it can also be stuffed.

Arbol Chili A dried chili, bright red in color, that is extremely hot. The chili is thin and about 2½ inches long.

Mulato Chili Similar to the ancho chili in appearance, the mulato chili is less wrinkled and is black-brown in color. It is somewhat sweeter in flavor than the ancho chili.

Pasilla Chili Quite hot and rich in flavor, this long, narrow chili is wrinkled and a dark black-brown in color.

Chilies, Fresh It is estimated that there are over 100 different varieties of chilies in Mexico; the types of chilies vary from region to region within the country. Each chili has its own flavor and degree of hotness, lending uniqueness to the dishes of a specific region. Select fresh chilies that are bright in color, shiny, unwrinkled, and firm. Chilies, if fresh, can be refrigerated 1 to 2 weeks. The veins and seeds of chilies are particularly hot—remove and discard them (using rubber gloves and protecting your eyes) unless the extra "fire" is desired!

Anaheim Chili A light green chili about 1½ inches in diameter and 5 to 6 inches long, with a rounded end. It is also called *chile verde* or New Mexico chili when dried. This chili can range from mild to hot in flavor, so taste before using.

Jalapeño Chili Probably the most well known Mexican chili in this country. The dark green jalapeño can be short or medium in length, and it is somewhat chubby with rounded ends. It is also available pickled in jars; the juice is often used in recipes, too.

Poblano Chili These black-green chilies have an irregular triangular shape, tapering to a point at the bottom. They are much larger than the jalapeño or serrano chilies, averaging 2 to 3 inches in width, 4 to 5 inches in length. These chilies, traditionally used to make chiles rellenos, can range in hotness from mild to very hot; they are often roasted before using in recipes.

Serrano Chili Also very well known here, the serrano is much thinner than the jalapeño, with pointed ends.

Cilantro   Sometimes called coriander, this aromatic herb (always used fresh in these recipes) is one that people either love or detest. The tender stems in the area of the leaves can be used as well as the leaves. The delicate flavor can be lost when cooked a long time, so add at the end of cooking or as a generous garnish. To store, place the bunch of cilantro in a glass of water, cover loosely with a plastic bag, and refrigerate.

Corn Husks   Available in large supermarkets and health food stores, the packaged husks will be flattened, trimmed, and ready to use. To soften them, soak in hot water as directed in the recipes.

Jicama   This crisp-textured vegetable is shaped much like a huge beet. It is covered with a tough brown skin that must be peeled away, and it can be eaten raw or cooked. Select jicamas that are firm and unwrinkled; if very fresh, they can be refrigerated 2 to 3 weeks.

Masa Harina   The Quaker Oats brand masa harina is available nationwide. The powdered meal is used for tamales; it should be stored airtight at room temperature. Fresh masa can be purchased at tortilla factories and large Mexican supermarkets.

Pepitas   These hulled, unsalted pumpkin seeds may be more readily purchased in health food stores than supermarkets. They are green and elongated in shape. They are wonderful toasted and used as a garnish and are also ground for use in sauces such as mole. Store at room temperature or in the freezer to prevent rancidity.

Pine Nuts   A rich-flavored nut also common in Italian and Mediterranean cuisines. Slivered almonds can be used as a substitute. Store in the freezer to prevent rancidity.

Plantains   These look like very large bananas. They are green when unripe and turn black and soft with yellow flesh when ripened. Most recipes require ripened plantains, and they are always eaten cooked. When green, they are impossible to peel without a sharp knife. To ripen green plantains, store in a brown paper bag in a dark place 5 to 7 days.

Tomatillos   Also called green tomatoes, they are not really a tomato but a cousin to the husked ground cherry. They are covered with a papery husk that needs to be removed; the fruit underneath is somewhat sticky. Tomatillos are seldom eaten raw. Used mostly in salsas and soups, the fruit has a tart flavor, which is often sweetened with a pinch of sugar.

White Cheese   *Queso blanco,* or *queso fresco,* is a fresh, firm cheese with a texture similar to feta. It crumbles readily and is slightly salty and acid in flavor. Feta or farmer's cheese can be substituted.

1
APPETIZERS

Red Tomato Salsa

Green Tomato Salsa

Black Bean Dip

Pinto Bean and Avocado Dip

Chile con Queso

Sombrero Dip

Baked Tortilla Chips

Queso Fundido

Nachos

Quesadillas

Tortilla Wedges

Beef Empanadas

Fried Green Plantains

Fried Ripe Plantains

Jicama with Lime and Cilantro

RED TOMATO SALSA

Poblano chilies can be quite hot in flavor, so taste before using; a green bell (sweet) pepper can be substituted if desired.

Serves 16 (about 2 tablespoons each)

2 large tomatoes, cut into wedges
1 small onion, finely chopped
1 small poblano chili, veins and seeds discarded, chopped
¼ jalapeño chili, seeds and veins discarded, chopped
1 clove garlic, minced
¼ cup loosely packed cilantro, finely chopped
   Salt, to taste
   Baked Tortilla Chips (see p. 9)

1. Process tomatoes, onion, chilies, and garlic in food processor or blender until finely chopped. Mix in cilantro; season to taste with salt.

2. Spoon Salsa into bowl; serve with Baked Tortilla Chips (not included in Nutritional Data).

Nutritional Data

PER SERVING		EXCHANGES	
Calories:	9	Milk:	0.0
% Calories from fat:	10	Vegetable:	0.5
Fat (gm):	0.1	Fruit:	0.0
Sat. fat (gm):	0	Bread:	0.0
Cholesterol (mg):	0	Meat:	0.0
Sodium (gm):	4	Fat:	0.0
Protein (gm):	0.4		
Carbohydrate (gm):	1.9		

GREEN TOMATO SALSA

Mexican green tomatoes (tomatillos) contain natural pectin, so the salsa will thicken when refrigerated. You can thin it to desired consistency with reserved cooking liquid or water.

Serves 16 (about 2 tablespoons each)

1½ pounds Mexican green tomatoes (*tomatillos*)
½ medium onion, finely chopped
2 cloves garlic, minced
¼ small jalapeño chili, seeds and veins discarded, very finely chopped
2 tablespoons finely chopped cilantro
½ teaspoon ground cumin
¼ teaspoon dried oregano leaves
⅛–¼ teaspoon sugar
Salt, to taste
Baked Tortilla Chips (see p. 9)

1. Remove and discard husks from tomatoes; simmer tomatoes in water to cover in large saucepan until tender, 5 to 8 minutes. Cool; drain, reserving liquid.

2. Process tomatoes, onion, garlic, jalapeño chili, cilantro, cumin, and oregano in food processor or blender, using pulse technique, until almost smooth, adding enough reserved liquid to make medium dipping consistency. Add sugar. Season to taste with salt.

3. Spoon salsa into bowl; serve with Baked Tortilla Chips (not included in Nutritional Data).

Nutritional Data

PER SERVING		EXCHANGES	
Calories:	17	Milk:	0.0
% Calories from fat:	22	Vegetable:	0.5
Fat (gm):	0.5	Fruit:	0.0
Sat. fat (gm):	0	Bread:	0.0
Cholesterol (mg):	0	Meat:	0.0
Sodium (gm):	2	Fat:	0.0
Protein (gm):	0.5		
Carbohydrate (gm):	3.1		

BLACK BEAN DIP

If a chunkier dip is desired, coarsely mash 1/2 cup of the total beans and reserve. Make dip as directed, then stir the mashed beans into the dip. Purchased baked tortilla chips can be substituted for the homemade chips in the recipe.

Serves 12 (about 2 tablespoons each)

Vegetable cooking spray
1/2 cup thinly sliced green onions and tops
1–2 cloves garlic, minced
1 can (15 ounces) black beans, rinsed, drained
3/4 cup (3 ounces) shredded reduced-fat Cheddar cheese
1/4 teaspoon salt
1/3 cup vegetable broth, or water
1–2 tablespoons finely chopped cilantro
Baked Tortilla Chips (see p. 9)

1. Spray small skillet with cooking spray; heat over medium heat until hot. Saute onions and garlic until tender, about 3 minutes.

2. Process black beans, cheese, and salt in food processor or blender until almost smooth, adding enough broth to make desired dipping consistency. Mix in onion mixture and cilantro.

3. Spoon dip into bowl; serve with Baked Tortilla Chips (not included in Nutritional Data).

Nutritional Data

PER SERVING		EXCHANGES	
Calories:	48	Milk:	0.0
% Calories from fat:	21	Vegetable:	0.0
Fat (gm):	1.3	Fruit:	0.0
Sat. fat (gm):	0.5	Bread:	0.5
Cholesterol (mg):	3.8	Meat:	0.0
Sodium (gm):	254	Fat:	0.0
Protein (gm):	4.5		
Carbohydrate (gm):	7		

PINTO BEAN AND AVOCADO DIP

Avocado and tomato brighten this well-flavored bean dip. Increase the amount of jalapeño chili if you dare—or use the seeds and veins for maximum hotness.

Serves 12 (about 2 tablespoons each)

1 can (15 ounces) pinto beans, rinsed, drained
3/4 cup finely chopped onion
2 cloves garlic
1/2 jalapeño chili, seeds and veins discarded, minced
3 tablespoons finely chopped cilantro
1 large tomato, chopped
1/2 medium avocado, peeled, pitted, chopped
2–3 tablespoons medium or hot prepared salsa
Salt and pepper, to taste
Baked Tortilla Chips (see p. 9)

1. Process beans in food processor or blender until smooth; add onion, garlic, jalapeño chili, and cilantro. Process, using pulse technique, until blended. Mix in tomato, avocado, and salsa; season to taste with salt and pepper. Refrigerate 1 to 2 hours for flavors to blend.

2. Spoon dip into serving bowl; serve with Baked Tortilla Chips (not included in Nutritional Data).

Nutritional Data

PER SERVING		EXCHANGES	
Calories:	54	Milk:	0.0
% Calories from fat:	25	Vegetable:	0.5
Fat (gm):	1.7	Fruit:	0.0
Sat. fat (gm):	0	Bread:	0.5
Cholesterol (mg):	0	Meat:	0.0
Sodium (gm):	153	Fat:	0.0
Protein (gm):	3		
Carbohydrate (gm):	8.3		

CHILE CON QUESO

◆

This popular dip is generally made with full-fat Mexican chihuahua, Monterey Jack, Muenster, or Cheddar cheese. Our "skinny" version is made with reduced-fat pasteurized processed cheese product for creamy texture and fat-free Cheddar cheese for added flavor.

Serves 12 (about 2 tablespoons each)

Vegetable cooking spray
5 medium anaheim, or 2 medium poblano, chilies, seeds and veins discarded, cut into halves
1 small onion, chopped
1 small tomato, chopped
½ teaspoon dried oregano leaves
2 cups (8 ounces) reduced-fat pasteurized processed cheese product, shredded
1 cup (4 ounces) shredded fat-free Cheddar cheese
2–4 tablespoons skim milk
Baked Tortilla Chips (see p. 9)

1. Line jellyroll pan with aluminum foil; spray with cooking spray. Place chilies, skin sides up, on pan. Bake at 425 degrees until chilies are browned and soft, 20 to 25 minutes. Cool slightly; cut into strips.

2. Spray small saucepan with cooking spray; heat over medium heat until hot. Saute onion, tomato, and oregano until onion is tender, about 5 minutes. Add cheeses and chilies; cook over low heat until melted, stirring in milk for desired consistency.

3. Serve warm in serving bowl with Baked Tortilla Chips (not included in Nutritional Data) for dipping.

Nutritional Data

PER SERVING		EXCHANGES	
Calories:	70	Milk:	0.0
% Calories from fat:	26	Vegetable:	1.0
Fat (gm):	2.1	Fruit:	0.0
Sat. fat (gm):	1.4	Bread:	0.0
Cholesterol (mg):	8.5	Meat:	1.0
Sodium (gm):	355	Fat:	0.0
Protein (gm):	7.8		
Carbohydrate (gm):	5.9		

Sombrero Dip

The ingredients in this appetizer dip are layered in smaller and smaller circles, resembling the top of a sombrero when finished! Use Florida avocados for making the Guacamole, as they are lower in fat than California avocados!

Serves 6

Vegetable cooking spray
1/4 cup chopped poblano chili, or green bell pepper
1/4 cup chopped onion
4–5 leaves romaine lettuce
1 1/2 cups Refried Beans (see p. 102), or 1 can (15 ounces) vegetarian refried beans
1/2 cup Red Tomato Salsa (see p. 2), or prepared salsa
1/2 cup cooked, crumbled Chorizo (see p. 70)
1/2 cup chopped romaine lettuce
1/2 cup chopped tomato
Guacamole (recipe follows)
1/4 cup (1 ounce) shredded fat-free Cheddar cheese
1/2 cup fat-free sour cream
1 green onion and top, thinly sliced
Baked Tortilla Chips (see p. 9)

1. Spray small skillet with cooking spray; heat over medium heat until hot. Saute poblano chili and onion until tender, 3 to 5 minutes; reserve.

2. Line a dinner-size serving plate with lettuce leaves; spoon on Refried Beans in a ring, 2 inches from edge of lettuce. Spoon Red Tomato Salsa over beans, leaving edge of bean ring showing.

3. Combine Chorizo and reserved sauteed chili and onion; sprinkle over salsa. Sprinkle chopped lettuce and tomato over Chorizo mixture, leaving edge of Chorizo ring showing.

4. Spoon Guacamole over lettuce and tomato, leaving edge of ring showing; sprinkle with Cheddar cheese. Spoon sour cream in large dollop on top; sprinkle with green onion. Serve with Baked Tortilla Chips (not included in Nutritional Data) for dipping.

Guacamole

1 medium Florida avocado (about 5 ounces),
  peeled, pitted
½ small onion, finely chopped
½ small jalapeño chili, seeds and veins discarded,
  minced
1–2 teaspoons finely chopped cilantro
  Salt and white pepper, to taste

1. Coarsely mash avocado in small bowl (mixture should be chunky, rather than smooth). Mix in onion, jalapeño chili, and cilantro. Season to taste with salt and pepper. Makes about ⅔ cup.

Nutritional Data

PER SERVING		EXCHANGES	
Calories:	136	Milk:	0.0
% Calories from fat:	19	Vegetable:	2.0
Fat (gm):	3	Fruit:	0.0
Sat. fat (gm):	0.7	Bread:	0.5
Cholesterol (mg):	9	Meat:	0.5
Sodium (gm):	111	Fat:	0.5
Protein (gm):	10		
Carbohydrate (gm):	18.8		

BAKED TORTILLA CHIPS

Make these chips with either flour or corn tortillas, using any combination of the suggested spices. Store at room temperature in an airtight container.

Serves 6 (8 chips each)

6 flour or corn tortillas (see separate Nutritional Data)
Vegetable cooking spray
1/2 teaspoon total of desired herbs: ground cumin, chili powder, paprika, dried oregano leaves
Salt, to taste
Cayenne pepper, to taste

1. Cut each tortilla into 8 wedges; arrange in single layer on jellyroll pan. Spray tortillas with cooking spray. Sprinkle lightly with herbs, salt, and cayenne pepper.

2. Bake at 350 degrees until lightly browned, 5 to 7 minutes.

Nutritional Data *(using flour tortillas)*

PER SERVING		EXCHANGES	
Calories:	84	Milk:	0.0
% Calories from fat:	21	Vegetable:	0.0
Fat (gm):	1.9	Fruit:	0.0
Sat. fat (gm):	0.3	Bread:	1.0
Cholesterol (mg):	0	Meat:	0.0
Sodium (gm):	122	Fat:	0.0
Protein (gm):	2.2		
Carbohydrate (gm):	14.3		

Nutritional Data *(using corn tortillas)*

PER SERVING		EXCHANGES	
Calories:	58	Milk:	0.0
% Calories from fat:	11	Vegetable:	0.0
Fat (gm):	0.7	Fruit:	0.0
Sat. fat (gm):	0.1	Bread:	0.5
Cholesterol (mg):	0	Meat:	0.0
Sodium (gm):	43	Fat:	0.0
Protein (gm):	1.5		
Carbohydrate (gm):	12		

QUESO FUNDIDO

This melted cheese mixture is spooned onto warm tortillas, topped with a sprinkling of Chorizo, onion, and cilantro, and rolled—tuck up the end for easy eating! The Chorizo used is about ¼ of the recipe; freeze the remaining Chorizo to use for another meal.

Serves 8

Vegetable cooking spray
¼ cup chopped red bell pepper
¾ cup (3 ounces) shredded fat-free Cheddar cheese
½ cup (2 ounces) cubed reduced-fat pasteurized processed cheese product
¼–⅓ cup skim milk
8 corn tortillas, warm
½ cup cooked, crumbled Chorizo (see p. 70)
2 tablespoons finely chopped green onions and tops
2 tablespoons finely chopped cilantro

1. Spray small saucepan with cooking spray; heat over medium heat until hot. Saute red bell pepper until tender, 2 to 3 minutes. Add cheeses; cook over low heat until melted, stirring in milk for desired consistency.

2. Spoon about 2 tablespoons cheese mixture in the center of each tortilla. Sprinkle with Chorizo, green onions, and cilantro and roll up.

Nutritional Data

PER SERVING		EXCHANGES	
Calories:	106	Milk:	0.0
% Calories from fat:	15	Vegetable:	0.0
Fat (gm):	1.8	Fruit:	0.0
Sat. fat (gm):	0.7	Bread:	1.0
Cholesterol (mg):	10.7	Meat:	1.0
Sodium (gm):	265	Fat:	0.0
Protein (gm):	9		
Carbohydrate (gm):	14		

NACHOS

---

*A favorite, but high-fat and -calorie restaurant appetizer that can
be made in a healthy "skinny" version at home! Canned refried
beans can be substituted for the pinto beans, and purchased
baked tortilla chips and salsa can be substituted for the
homemade. Cooked, crumbled Chorizo (see p. 70) can be added
to make these nachos grandes!*

Serves 6

Baked Tortilla Chips, made with corn tortillas
(see p. 9)

1 can (15 1/2 ounces) pinto beans, rinsed, drained,
coarsely mashed

1 cup Red Tomato Salsa, or Green Tomato Salsa
(see pp. 2 and 3), divided

1/2–1 teaspoon chili powder

3/4 teaspoon dried oregano leaves

2–3 cloves garlic, minced

Salt, to taste

1/2 cup (2 ounces) shredded reduced-fat Cheddar,
or Monterey Jack, cheese

1 medium tomato, chopped

1/2 small avocado, chopped

2 green onions and tops, sliced

6 pitted ripe olives, sliced (optional)

1/4 cup fat-free sour cream

1. Spread Baked Tortilla Chips in a single layer in jellyroll pan. Mix beans,
   1/4 cup Salsa, chili powder, oregano, and garlic; season to taste with
   salt. Spoon refried beans over tortilla chips; sprinkle with cheese. Bake
   at 350 degrees until beans are hot and cheese melted, 5 to 10 minutes.

2. Sprinkle with tomato, avocado, onions, and olives; garnish with dollops
   of sour cream. Serve with remaining Salsa.

Nutritional Data

PER SERVING		EXCHANGES	
Calories:	200	Milk:	0.0
% Calories from fat:	22	Vegetable:	1.0
Fat (gm):	5.4	Fruit:	0.0
Sat. fat (gm):	1.2	Bread:	2.0
Cholesterol (mg):	5.1	Meat:	0.0
Sodium (gm):	455	Fat:	1.0
Protein (gm):	10.5		
Carbohydrate (gm):	32.5		

QUESADILLAS

The simplest quesadillas are made only with cheese. Our version adds the Mexican poblano chili, onion, and cilantro; Chorizo (see p. 70) would be a flavorful addition.

Serves 6

Vegetable cooking spray
1 poblano chili, or green bell pepper, sliced
1 medium onion, finely chopped
1 teaspoon ground cumin
2 tablespoons finely chopped cilantro
1 cup (4 ounces) shredded reduced-fat Cheddar cheese
6 flour tortillas
3/4 cup Red or Green Tomato Salsa (see pp. 2 and 3)
6 tablespoons fat-free sour cream

1. Spray large skillet with cooking spray; heat over medium heat until hot. Saute poblano chili, onion, and cumin until vegetables are tender, 3 to 5 minutes; stir in cilantro.

2. Sprinkle cheese on half of each tortilla; spoon vegetable mixture over. Fold tortillas in half.

3. Spray large skillet with cooking spray; heat over medium heat until hot. Cook quesadillas over medium to medium-high heat until browned on the bottoms, 2 to 3 minutes. Spray tops of quesadillas with cooking spray; turn and cook until browned on the other side. Cut into wedges and serve warm with Salsa and sour cream.

Nutritional Data

PER SERVING		EXCHANGES	
Calories:	165	Milk:	0.0
% Calories from fat:	26	Vegetable:	1.5
Fat (gm):	4.8	Fruit:	0.0
Sat. fat (gm):	1.7	Bread:	1.0
Cholesterol (mg):	10.1	Meat:	0.5
Sodium (gm):	393	Fat:	0.5
Protein (gm):	8.3		
Carbohydrate (gm):	22.9		

TORTILLA WEDGES

◆

Fun to make and eat—our Mexican-style version of pizza!

Serves 12 (2 wedges each)

Vegetable cooking spray
Chorizo (see p. 70)
½ cup chopped green bell pepper
½ cup chopped onion
4 large flour tortillas (10-inch)
1 cup (4 ounces) shredded reduced-fat Monterey
  Jack cheese
1 cup (4 ounces) shredded fat-free Cheddar
  cheese
1 cup Red Tomato Salsa (see p. 2) or prepared
  salsa
¾ cup fat-free sour cream

1. Spray medium skillet with cooking spray; heat over medium heat until hot. Add Chorizo and cook over medium heat until brown, crumbling with fork; add green pepper and onion and cook until tender, 2 to 3 minutes.

2. Place tortillas on baking sheets; sprinkle evenly with Monterey Jack cheese. Sprinkle with Chorizo mixture, and top with Cheddar cheese. Bake at 450 degrees until edges of tortillas are browned and cheese is melted, 6 to 8 minutes. Top with Red Tomato Salsa and sour cream. Cut each tortilla into 6 wedges.

Nutritional Data

PER SERVING		EXCHANGES	
Calories:	135	Milk:	0.0
% Calories from fat:	24	Vegetable:	0.5
Fat (gm):	3.7	Fruit:	0.0
Sat. fat (gm):	1.5	Bread:	0.5
Cholesterol (mg):	24.8	Meat:	1.5
Sodium (gm):	313	Fat:	0.0
Protein (gm):	14.4		
Carbohydrate (gm):	11.4		

BEEF EMPANADAS

Pork tenderloin or chicken breast can be substituted for the beef in this recipe. The raisins and spices lend a sweet flavor to the traditional meat filling.

Serves 10 (3 empanadas each)

12 ounces boneless beef eye of round steak
   Vegetable cooking spray
¼ cup finely chopped onion
3 cloves garlic, minced
2 small tomatoes, finely chopped
⅓ cup raisins
2 tablespoons slivered almonds (optional)
1 tablespoon cider vinegar
½ teaspoon ground cinnamon
⅛ teaspoon ground cloves
3 tablespoons finely chopped cilantro
   Salt and pepper, to taste
   Empanada Pastry (recipe follows)
2 tablespoons skim milk

1. Cut beef into 2-inch cubes and place in saucepan with 2 inches of water; heat to boiling. Reduce heat and simmer, covered, until beef is tender, about 15 minutes. Drain, reserving meat and ½ cup broth. Shred beef finely.

2. Spray large skillet with cooking spray; heat over medium heat until hot. Saute onion and garlic until tender, about 5 minutes. Add reserved beef and broth, tomatoes, raisins, almonds, vinegar, cinnamon, and cloves; cook over medium heat until broth has

evaporated but mixture is still moist, about 10 minutes. Stir in cilantro; season to taste with salt and pepper.

3. Roll half of the Pastry on floured surface to ⅛ inch thickness; cut into 3-inch rounds with cookie cutter. Place scant tablespoon of meat mixture on each piece of pastry. Brush edges of pastry with water; fold in half and crimp edges firmly by hand or with tines of a fork. Make slit in top of each pastry with a sharp knife. Repeat with remaining pastry and meat mixture. Brush tops of pastries lightly with milk.

4. Bake empanadas on sprayed cookie sheets at 400 degrees until golden, 15 to 20 minutes. Serve warm. Makes about 30.

Empanada Pastry

1¼	cups all-purpose flour
1	tablespoon sugar
¼	teaspoon baking powder
⅛	teaspoon salt
3	tablespoons vegetable shortening
1	teaspoon lemon juice, or distilled white vinegar
3–4	tablespoons skim milk, or water

1. Combine flour, sugar, baking powder, and salt in small bowl; cut in shortening until mixture resembles coarse crumbs. Mix in lemon juice and milk, a tablespoon at a time, to form soft dough. Refrigerate until ready to use.

Nutritional Data

PER SERVING		EXCHANGES	
Calories:	159	Milk:	0.0
% Calories from fat:	29	Vegetable:	0.0
Fat (gm):	5.1	Fruit:	0.0
Sat. fat (gm):	1.5	Bread:	0.5
Cholesterol (mg):	16.5	Meat:	0.5
Sodium (gm):	57	Fat:	0.0
Protein (gm):	8.7		
Carbohydrate (gm):	19.5		

FRIED GREEN PLANTAINS

*Most often eaten when ripe and soft, this delectable snack
is made with unripe plantains.*

Serves 4

2 unripe green plantains
Vegetable oil
Salt, to taste

1. Cut plantains into 3-inch lengths; cut through skin to fruit and peel skin away. Cut plantains into ¼-inch slices.

2. Heat 1½ to 2 inches of oil to 350 degrees in large saucepan. Fry plantains until golden on both sides; drain well on paper toweling. Let cool slightly; flatten plantain slices with fist or mallet.

3. Heat oil to 375 degrees; fry plantain slices again, about 1 minute on each side. Drain well on paper toweling; sprinkle lightly with salt and arrange in a bowl. Serve hot.

Nutritional Data

PER SERVING		EXCHANGES	
Calories:	119	Milk:	0.0
% Calories from fat:	10	Vegetable:	0.0
Fat (gm):	1.5	Fruit:	2.0
Sat. fat (gm):	0.3	Bread:	0.0
Cholesterol (mg):	0	Meat:	0.0
Sodium (gm):	4	Fat:	0.0
Protein (gm):	1.2		
Carbohydrate (gm):	28.6		

FRIED RIPE PLANTAINS

When ripe, the plantain skin is black and the fruit is soft. If purchasing plantains when green, they will ripen more quickly if kept in a closed paper bag in a dark place.

Serves 4

Vegetable oil
2 ripe plantains, peeled, diagonally cut into
 ¼-inch slices
Salt, to taste

1. Heat 1½ to 2 inches of oil to 375 degrees in large saucepan. Fry plantains until golden on both sides; drain well on paper toweling.

2. Sprinkle plantains with salt and arrange in a bowl; serve hot.

 Note: For a sweet variation, plantains can be sprinkled with sugar and cinnamon instead of salt.

Nutritional Data

PER SERVING		EXCHANGES	
Calories:	119	Milk:	0.0
% Calories from fat:	10	Vegetable:	0.0
Fat (gm):	1.5	Fruit:	2.0
Sat. fat (gm):	0.3	Bread:	0.0
Cholesterol (mg):	0	Meat:	0.0
Sodium (gm):	4	Fat:	0.0
Protein (gm):	1.2		
Carbohydrate (gm):	28.6		

JICAMA WITH LIME AND CILANTRO

Very simple, and incredibly tasty!

Serves 4

1 medium jicama, peeled, thinly sliced
Salt, to taste
Lime juice, to taste
1–2 tablespoons finely chopped cilantro

1. Arrange jicama slices on large serving plate; sprinkle very lightly with salt. Then sprinkle with lime juice and cilantro.

Nutritional Data

PER SERVING		EXCHANGES	
Calories:	17	Milk:	0.0
% Calories from fat:	2	Vegetable:	1.0
Fat (gm):	0	Fruit:	0.0
Sat. fat (gm):	0	Bread:	0.0
Cholesterol (mg):	0	Meat:	0.0
Sodium (gm):	0	Fat:	0.0
Protein (gm):	0.5		
Carbohydrate (gm):	3.8		

2
SOUPS

Tortilla Soup

Pozole

Poblano Chili Soup

Creamed Corn Soup

Garlic Soup with Toast

Black Bean Soup

Gazpacho

Chayote Squash Soup with Cilantro Cream

Shrimp and Black Bean Soup

Garbanzo Bean Soup

Meatball Soup

Sweet Red Pepper Soup

TORTILLA SOUP

Add the tortilla strips to the soup just before serving so they are crisp. If desired, the tortilla strips can be baked on a cookie sheet at 350 degrees until browned and crisp, about 5 minutes. The soup should be slightly piquant— add additional lime juice to taste.

Serves 6 (main dish servings; about 1½ cups each)

Vegetable cooking spray
3 corn, or flour, tortillas, cut into 2 x ¼-inch strips
1 small onion, chopped
1 cup chopped celery
1 medium tomato, coarsely chopped
½ teaspoon dried basil leaves
½ teaspoon ground cumin
5 cups fat-free, reduced-sodium chicken broth
1 can (15 ½ ounces) pinto beans rinsed and drained
6 ounces shredded cooked chicken breast (no skin)
2 teaspoons finely chopped cilantro
1–2 teaspoons lime juice
Salt, to taste
Cayenne pepper, to taste

1. Spray medium skillet with cooking spray; heat over medium heat until hot. Add tortillas; spray tortillas with cooking spray and cook over medium heat, tossing occasionally, until browned and crisp, about 5 minutes. Reserve.

2. Spray large saucepan with cooking spray; heat over medium heat until hot. Saute onion, celery, tomato, basil, and cumin until onion is tender, 3 to 5 minutes. Add chicken broth, beans, and chicken; heat to boiling. Reduce heat and simmer, uncovered, 3 to 5 minutes. Stir in cilantro; season with lime juice, and add salt and pepper to taste.

3. Add tortilla strips to soup bowls and ladle on soup.

Nutritional Data

PER SERVING		EXCHANGES	
Calories:	176	Milk:	0.0
% Calories from fat:	10	Vegetable:	1.0
Fat (gm):	2	Fruit:	0.0
Sat. fat (gm):	0.3	Bread:	1.0
Cholesterol (mg):	24.1	Meat:	2.0
Sodium (gm):	386	Fat:	0.0
Protein (gm):	19.1		
Carbohydrate (gm):	22.6		

POZOLE

Traditionally, this soup is made with a pig's head or pork hocks; our version contains lean pork tenderloin and chicken breast instead. The soup always contains hominy and is served with a variety of crisp vegetable garnishes.

Serves 6 (main dish servings; about 1⅓ cups each)

- 2 ancho chilies, stems, seeds, and veins discarded
- 1 cup boiling water
  Vegetable cooking spray
- ½ cup chopped onion
- 1 clove garlic, minced
- 2 cans (14½ ounces each) fat-free, reduced-sodium chicken broth
- 8 ounces pork tenderloin, cut into 1-inch pieces
- 8 ounces skinless, boneless chicken breast, cut into 1-inch pieces
- 1 can (15½ ounces) hominy, rinsed, drained
- 1 can (14½ ounces) reduced-sodium tomatoes, drained, coarsely chopped
- ½ teaspoon dried oregano leaves
- ¼ teaspoon dried thyme leaves
  Salt and pepper, to taste
- 4 lime wedges
- ¼ cup each, thinly sliced: lettuce, cabbage, green onion, radishes, and shredded carrots

1. Cover chilies with boiling water in small bowl; let stand until softened, about 10 minutes. Process chilies and water in food processor or blender until smooth.

2. Spray large saucepan with vegetable cooking spray; heat over medium heat until hot. Saute onion and garlic until tender; add chicken broth and meats and heat to boiling. Reduce heat and simmer, covered, until meats are tender, 10 to 15 minutes; strain, returning broth to saucepan. Shred meats with fork.

3. Add meats, hominy, tomatoes, oregano, and thyme to saucepan; cook, covered, over low heat 10 to 15 minutes. Season to taste with salt and pepper.

4. Serve soup in bowls; squeeze juice from one lime wedge into each bowl. Pass fresh vegetables for each person to add to soup.

Nutritional Data

PER SERVING		EXCHANGES	
Calories:	181	Milk:	0.0
% Calories from fat:	16	Vegetable:	1.0
Fat (gm):	3.2	Fruit:	0.0
Sat. fat (gm):	0.9	Bread:	1.0
Cholesterol (mg):	44.8	Meat:	2.5
Sodium (gm):	244	Fat:	0.0
Protein (gm):	21.2		
Carbohydrate (gm):	16.7		

POBLANO CHILI SOUP

◆

Poblano chilies give this soup its extraordinary flavor. Readily available in most large supermarkets, they can vary in flavor from mild to very picante. Taste the peppers before making this soup; if they are too hot for your taste, substitute some green bell peppers and decrease the amount of jalapeño.

Serves 6 (about 1 cup each)

Vegetable cooking spray
2 medium onions, chopped
4 medium poblano chilies, seeds and veins
   discarded, chopped
½–1 small jalapeño chili, seeds and veins discarded,
   finely chopped
2 cans (14½ ounces each) fat-free, reduced-
   sodium chicken, or vegetable, broth
3 cups tomato juice
½ teaspoon ground cumin
½–1 cup water, divided
Salt and pepper, to taste
Minced cilantro, as garnish

1. Spray large saucepan with cooking spray; heat over medium heat until hot. Saute onions and chilies until onions are tender, about 5 minutes. Add broth; heat to boiling. Reduce heat and simmer, covered, until chilies are very tender, about 5 minutes.

2. Process broth mixture in food processor or blender until smooth; return to saucepan. Add tomato juice, cumin, and enough water for desired consistency; heat to boiling. Reduce heat and simmer, uncovered, 10 minutes. Season to taste with salt and pepper. Serve soup in bowls; sprinkle with cilantro.

Nutritional Data

PER SERVING		EXCHANGES	
Calories:	88	Milk:	0.0
% Calories from fat:	3	Vegetable:	3.5
Fat (gm):	0.4	Fruit:	0.0
Sat. fat (gm):	0	Bread:	0.0
Cholesterol (mg):	0	Meat:	0.0
Sodium (gm):	498	Fat:	0.0
Protein (gm):	6.4		
Carbohydrate (gm):	18.2		

CREAMED CORN SOUP

Garnish this colorful soup with a sprinkling of finely chopped cilantro or parsley.

Serves 6 (about 1 cup each)

Vegetable cooking spray
½ cup chopped onion
1 medium Idaho potato, peeled, cubed
2 cloves garlic, minced
1 can (15½ ounces) whole kernel corn, drained
3 tablespoons all-purpose flour
½ teaspoon ground coriander
⅛ teaspoon cayenne pepper
2 cans (14½ ounces each) vegetable broth
1 cup skim milk
2 medium tomatoes, chopped
Salt and pepper, to taste
Paprika, as garnish

1. Spray a large saucepan with cooking spray; heat over medium heat until hot. Saute onion, potato, and garlic until onion is tender, about 5 minutes. Stir in corn, flour, coriander, and cayenne pepper; cook 1 to 2 minutes, stirring frequently. Stir in broth and heat to boiling; reduce heat and simmer, covered, until potato is tender, about 10 minutes.

2. Process mixture in food processor or blender until almost smooth; return to saucepan. Stir in milk and tomatoes; heat just to boiling. Reduce heat and simmer, uncovered, 5 minutes. Season to taste with salt and pepper. Serve soup in bowls; sprinkle with paprika.

Nutritional Data

PER SERVING		EXCHANGES	
Calories:	144	Milk:	0.0
% Calories from fat:	6	Vegetable:	0.0
Fat (gm):	1	Fruit:	0.0
Sat. fat (gm):	0.2	Bread:	2.0
Cholesterol (mg):	0.7	Meat:	0.0
Sodium (gm):	313	Fat:	0.0
Protein (gm):	5.2		
Carbohydrate (gm):	31.2		

GARLIC SOUP WITH TOAST

Traditionally, a whole beaten egg is slowly stirred into the simmering soup before serving, similar to Chinese egg drop soup. Try this if you don't mind the extra cholesterol.

Serves 4 (about 1 cup each)

4 slices firm bread (French or sourdough)
Vegetable cooking spray
1 tablespoon vegetable oil
6–8 cloves garlic, finely chopped
½ teaspoon ground cumin
¼ teaspoon ground oregano
¼ teaspoon cayenne pepper
2 cans (14½ ounces each) fat-free, reduced-sodium chicken broth
Salt, to taste
Cilantro, finely chopped, as garnish

1. Spray both sides of bread slices generously with cooking spray; cook in large skillet, over medium heat, until golden on both sides. Keep warm.

2. Heat oil in medium saucepan until hot; add garlic and cook over low heat until garlic is very soft and very lightly browned, 5 to 8 minutes. Stir in cumin, oregano, and cayenne pepper; cook 1 to 2 minutes. Add broth to saucepan; heat to boiling. Reduce heat and simmer, covered, 5 minutes. Season to taste with salt.

3. Place slices of bread in bottoms of 4 shallow bowls; ladle soup over. Sprinkle with cilantro.

Nutritional Data

PER SERVING		EXCHANGES	
Calories:	124	Milk:	0.0
% Calories from fat:	30	Vegetable:	0.0
Fat (gm):	4.3	Fruit:	0.0
Sat. fat (gm):	0.6	Bread:	1.0
Cholesterol (mg):	0	Meat:	0.0
Sodium (gm):	216	Fat:	1.0
Protein (gm):	6.8		
Carbohydrate (gm):	14.7		

BLACK BEAN SOUP

Dried beans can also be "quick cooked" rather than soaked over night before cooking. Place beans in a large saucepan and cover with 2 inches of water; heat to boiling and boil 2 minutes. Remove from heat and let stand 1 hour; drain and continue with step 2 in recipe below. Or, substitute three cans (15 ounces each) of rinsed and drained canned black beans for the dried.

Serves 4 (about 1¼ cups each)

1½ cups dried black beans
    Vegetable cooking spray
  1 large onion, chopped
  4 cloves garlic, minced
  1 tomato, chopped
  1 teaspoon dried oregano leaves
½ teaspoon dried thyme leaves
    Salt and pepper, to taste
  6 tablespoons fat-free sour cream
    Oregano or parsley, finely chopped, as garnish

1. Wash and sort beans, discarding any stones. Cover beans with 4 inches of water in a large saucepan; soak overnight and drain.

2. Spray large saucepan with cooking spray; heat over medium heat until hot. Saute onion and garlic 2 to 3 minutes; add tomato and herbs and cook 2 to 3 minutes longer. Add beans to saucepan; cover with 2 inches of water and heat to boiling. Reduce heat and simmer, covered, until beans are very tender, 1½ to 2 hours, adding water to cover beans if necessary. Drain mixture, reserving liquid.

3. Process bean mixture in food processor or blender until smooth, adding enough reserved cooking liquid to make desired consistency. Return soup to saucepan; heat over medium heat until hot through, 3 to 4 minutes. Season to taste with salt and pepper.

4. Serve soup in bowls; top each with a dollop of sour cream and sprinkle with oregano or parsley.

Nutritional Data

PER SERVING		EXCHANGES	
Calories:	200	Milk:	0.0
% Calories from fat:	4	Vegetable:	1.0
Fat (gm):	0.9	Fruit:	0.0
Sat. fat (gm):	0.2	Bread:	2.0
Cholesterol (mg):	0	Meat:	0.5
Sodium (gm):	20	Fat:	0.0
Protein (gm):	13.8		
Carbohydrate (gm):	39		

GAZPACHO

Gazpacho is Spanish in origin, but popularly served throughout Mexico and South America. Easy to make and served cold, this is a wonderful soup to keep on hand in summer months.

Serves 6 (about 1¼ cups each)

5 large tomatoes, divided
2 cups reduced-sodium tomato juice
2 cloves garlic
2 tablespoons lime juice
1 teaspoon dried oregano leaves
1 small seedless cucumber, coarsely chopped
1 cup chopped yellow bell pepper
1 cup chopped celery
6 green onions and tops, thinly sliced, divided
2 tablespoons finely chopped cilantro
Salt and pepper, to taste
Avocado Sour Cream (recipe follows)
Hot pepper sauce (optional)

1. Cut tomatoes into halves; remove and discard seeds. Chop tomatoes, reserving 1 cup. Process remaining tomatoes, tomato juice, garlic, lime juice, and oregano in food processor or blender until smooth.

2. Mix tomato mixture, reserved tomatoes, cucumber, yellow bell pepper, celery, 5 green onions, and cilantro in a large bowl; season to taste with salt and pepper. Refrigerate until chilled, 3 to 4 hours.

3. Serve soup in chilled bowls; top each with a dollop of Avocado Sour Cream and sprinkle with remaining green onion. Serve with hot pepper sauce if desired.

Avocado Sour Cream

1/2 medium avocado, peeled, pitted, chopped
1/4 cup fat-free sour cream
 2 tablespoons skim milk
   Salt and white pepper, to taste

1. Process all ingredients in food processor until smooth; season to taste with salt and white pepper. Makes about 2/3 cup.

Nutritional Data

PER SERVING		EXCHANGES	
Calories:	76	Milk:	0.0
% Calories from fat:	17	Vegetable:	2.0
Fat (gm):	1.6	Fruit:	0.0
Sat. fat (gm):	0.3	Bread:	0.0
Cholesterol (mg):	0.1	Meat:	0.0
Sodium (gm):	46	Fat:	0.5
Protein (gm):	3.3		
Carbohydrate (gm):	15.1		

CHAYOTE SQUASH SOUP WITH CILANTRO CREAM

Chayote squash, often called a "vegetable pear," is native to Mexico. Readily available in supermarkets, the squash is light green in color and delicate in flavor.

Serves 6 (about 1 cup each)

   Vegetable cooking spray
 1 large onion, chopped
 2 cloves garlic, minced
 3 tablespoons flour
 3 large chayote squash, peeled, pitted, sliced
 3 cans (14 1/2 ounces each) fat-free, reduced-sodium chicken broth, divided
1/2 cup water
   Salt and white pepper, to taste
   Cilantro Cream (recipe follows)
   Cilantro, finely chopped, as garnish

1. Spray large saucepan with cooking spray; heat over medium heat until hot. Saute onion and garlic until tender, about 5 minutes. Stir in flour; cook over medium heat 2 minutes, stirring constantly.

2. Add squash and 1 can broth to saucepan; heat to boiling. Reduce heat and simmer, covered, until squash is tender, 15 to 20 minutes. Process mixture in food processor or blender until smooth; return to saucepan. Add remaining broth and water; season to taste with salt and white pepper. Heat over medium heat and serve warm, or refrigerate and serve chilled.

3. Serve soup in bowls; drizzle with Cilantro Cream and sprinkle with cilantro.

Cilantro Cream

⅓ cup fat-free sour cream
1 tablespoon finely chopped cilantro
¼–⅓ cup skim milk

1. Mix sour cream and cilantro in small bowl, adding enough milk for desired consistency. Makes about ½ cup.

Nutritional Data

PER SERVING		EXCHANGES	
Calories:	68	Milk:	0.0
% Calories from fat:	4	Vegetable:	2.0
Fat (gm):	0.3	Fruit:	0.0
Sat. fat (gm):	0.1	Bread:	0.0
Cholesterol (mg):	0.2	Meat:	0.5
Sodium (gm):	79	Fat:	0.0
Protein (gm):	6.8		
Carbohydrate (gm):	10.5		

SHRIMP AND BLACK BEAN SOUP

Authentically, leaves from the avocado tree are used for seasoning in this favorite Oaxacan soup. We've substituted a bay leaf, which is somewhat stronger in flavor.

Serves 6 (main dish servings; about 1½ cups each)

Vegetable cooking spray
2 medium onions, chopped
4 cloves garlic, minced
2 medium tomatoes, peeled, cut into wedges
3 cans (14½ ounces each) fat-free, reduced-sodium chicken broth, divided
½ cup water
3 cups cooked black beans, or 2 cans (15 ounces each) black beans, rinsed, drained
1 teaspoon ground cumin
1 teaspoon dried oregano leaves
1 teaspoon dried thyme leaves
1 bay leaf
8 ounces peeled, deveined shrimp
Salt and pepper, to taste
Cilantro, finely chopped, as garnish

1. Spray a large saucepan with cooking spray; heat over medium heat until hot. Saute onions and garlic until tender, about 5 minutes. Process onion mixture with tomatoes and 1 cup chicken broth until smooth; return to saucepan.

2. Add remaining broth, water, black beans, and herbs to saucepan; heat to boiling. Reduce heat and simmer, uncovered, 10 minutes, adding shrimp during last 5 minutes. Discard bay leaf and season to taste with salt and pepper.

3. Serve soup in bowls; sprinkle with cilantro.

Nutritional Data

PER SERVING		EXCHANGES	
Calories:	190	Milk:	0.0
% Calories from fat:	5	Vegetable:	1.0
Fat (gm):	1.1	Fruit:	0.0
Sat. fat (gm):	0.3	Bread:	1.5
Cholesterol (mg):	58.3	Meat:	1.5
Sodium (gm):	136	Fat:	0.0
Protein (gm):	19.1		
Carbohydrate (gm):	27		

GARBANZO BEAN SOUP

Garbanzo beans are more commonly found in the cuisine of central and southern Mexico.

Serves 4 (main dish servings; about 1¼ cups each)

Vegetable cooking spray
2 medium onions, chopped
2 cloves garlic, minced
2 cans (15¼ ounces each) garbanzo beans, rinsed, drained
2 cans (14½ ounces each) fat-free, reduced-sodium chicken broth, divided
1 teaspoon ground cumin
½–¾ teaspoon dried thyme leaves
Salt and pepper, to taste
¼ cup fat-free sour cream
Paprika, or chili powder, as garnish

1. Spray large saucepan with cooking spray; heat over medium heat until hot. Saute onions and garlic until tender, about 5 minutes. Process onion mixture, garbanzo beans, and 1 can chicken broth in food processor or blender until smooth.

2. Return mixture to saucepan; add remaining broth, cumin, and thyme and heat to boiling. Reduce heat and simmer, covered, 5 minutes. Season to taste with salt and pepper.

3. Serve soup in bowls; top with dollops of sour cream and sprinkle with paprika.

Nutritional Data

PER SERVING		EXCHANGES	
Calories:	264	Milk:	0.0
% Calories from fat:	14	Vegetable:	0.0
Fat (gm):	4.1	Fruit:	0.0
Sat. fat (gm):	0.6	Bread:	3.0
Cholesterol (mg):	0	Meat:	1.0
Sodium (gm):	333	Fat:	0.0
Protein (gm):	16		
Carbohydrate (gm):	42.9		

MEATBALL SOUP

*A great favorite in Mexico, this soup is traditionally
seasoned with mint; we've offered oregano as an
addition (or alternative), if you like.*

Serves 4 (main dish servings; about 2 cups each)

Vegetable cooking spray
¼ cup chopped onion
2 cloves garlic, minced
1 small jalapeño chili, seeds and veins discarded, minced
1 tablespoon flour
2 cups reduced-sodium tomato juice
2 cups water
2 cans (14½ ounces each) fat-free, reduced-sodium chicken broth
3 medium carrots, sliced
2 medium zucchini, sliced
½ teaspoon dried mint leaves
1½–2 teaspoons dried oregano leaves
Meatballs (recipe follows)
Salt and pepper, to taste

1. Spray large saucepan with cooking spray; heat over medium heat until hot. Saute onion, garlic, and jalapeño chili until tender, about 5 minutes. Stir in flour; cook over medium heat 1 to 2 minutes.

2. Add tomato juice, water, chicken broth, carrots, zucchini, mint, and oregano to saucepan; heat to boiling. Add meatballs; reduce heat and simmer, covered, until vegetables are tender and meatballs are cooked, 10 to 15 minutes. Season to taste with salt and pepper. Serve in bowls.

Meatballs

1 pound ground boneless beef (eye of round)
1/4 cup cooked rice
1/3 cup finely chopped onion
1 clove garlic, minced
1/2 teaspoon dried mint leaves
1/4 teaspoon dried oregano
1/4 teaspoon ground cumin
1/2 teaspoon salt
1/4 teaspoon pepper

1. Mix all ingredients in bowl; form into 24 small meatballs. Refrigerate, covered, until ready to cook (no longer than 8 hours). Makes 24 meatballs.

Nutritional Data

PER SERVING		EXCHANGES	
Calories:	227	Milk:	0.0
% Calories from fat:	16	Vegetable:	3.0
Fat (gm):	4.1	Fruit:	0.0
Sat. fat (gm):	1.4	Bread:	0.0
Cholesterol (mg):	54.7	Meat:	3.0
Sodium (gm):	426	Fat:	0.0
Protein (gm):	28		
Carbohydrate (gm):	20.2		

SWEET RED PEPPER SOUP

◆

*Use jarred roasted peppers for this soup, or roast 2 medium
red bell (sweet) peppers yourself. To roast peppers, cut in half
and discard seeds. Place peppers, skin sides up, on aluminum
foil-lined jellyroll pan. Broil 4 inches from heat source until
skins are blackened. Place peppers in a plastic bag 5 minutes
to loosen skins, then peel and discard them.*

Serves 4 (about 1 cup each)

Vegetable cooking spray
1 medium onion, chopped
½ small jalapeño chili, seeds and veins discarded,
   minced
1 clove garlic, minced
1 jar (5 ounces) roasted red bell peppers,
   drained
1 cup reduced-sodium tomato juice
1 can (14½ ounces) vegetable broth
¼ teaspoon dried marjoram leaves
   Salt and pepper, to taste
¼ cup fat-free sour cream
1 small green onion and top, thinly sliced

1. Spray medium saucepan with cooking spray; heat over medium heat
   until hot. Saute onion, jalapeño chili, and garlic until tender.

2. Process onion mixture, red bell peppers, and tomato juice in food
   processor or blender until smooth. Return mixture to saucepan and
   add vegetable broth and marjoram; heat to boiling. Reduce heat and
   simmer, covered, 15 minutes. Season to taste with salt and pepper.

3. Serve soup warm, or refrigerate and serve cold. Top each serving with
   a dollop of sour cream and sprinkle with green onion.

Nutritional Data

PER SERVING		EXCHANGES	
Calories:	60	Milk:	0.0
% Calories from fat:	3	Vegetable:	2.0
Fat (gm):	0.2	Fruit:	0.0
Sat. fat (gm):	0	Bread:	0.0
Cholesterol (mg):	0	Meat:	0.0
Sodium (gm):	62	Fat:	0.0
Protein (gm):	2.8		
Carbohydrate (gm):	13.3		

3
TAMALES

Three-Chili Tamales

Chicken and Poblano Tamales

Beef and Pinto Bean Tamales

THREE-CHILI TAMALES

*Ancho chilies are fresh poblano chilies that have been dried.
Corn husks and masa harina (see Ingredients) can be purchased
in large supermarkets or Mexican groceries.*

Serves 4 (3 tamales each)

12 corn husks
   Hot water
2 ancho chilies, stems, seeds and veins
   discarded
1/3 cup boiling water
1 large poblano chili, seeds and veins discarded,
   chopped
1 can (4 ounces) chopped green chilies, drained
3/4 teaspoon dried oregano leaves
1/2 teaspoon dried thyme leaves
   Salt and pepper, to taste
   Tamale Dough (recipe follows)

1. Soak corn husks in hot water until softened, about 1 hour; drain well on paper toweling.

2. Crumble ancho chilies into bowl; pour 1/3 cup boiling water over and let stand until softened, 15 to 20 minutes. Cook ancho chilies and liquid, poblano chili, green chilies, and herbs over medium heat in medium skillet until chilies are tender, 5 to 8 minutes, stirring frequently. Season to taste with salt and pepper. Mix in Tamale Dough.

3. Spoon about 1/4 cup of tamale mixture onto center of each corn husk; fold sides of husks over filling. Tie ends of tamales, making "bundles."

4. Place tamales on steamer rack in saucepan with 2 inches of water. Steam, covered, 2 hours, adding more water to saucepan if necessary. Serve warm. Makes 12 tamales.

Tamale Dough

1 cup masa harina
3/4 teaspoon baking powder
1 1/2 tablespoons margarine, softened
1/4–1/2 teaspoon salt
1 cup fat-free, reduced-sodium chicken broth

1. Combine masa harina, baking powder, margarine, and salt; gradually stir in broth (mixture will be soft). Makes about 1 cup.

Nutritional Data

PER SERVING		EXCHANGES	
Calories:	176	Milk:	0.0
% Calories from fat:	27	Vegetable:	1.0
Fat (gm):	5.4	Fruit:	0.0
Sat. fat (gm):	1	Bread:	1.5
Cholesterol (mg):	0	Meat:	0.0
Sodium (gm):	400	Fat:	1.0
Protein (gm):	4.7		
Carbohydrate (gm):	28.3		

CHICKEN AND POBLANO TAMALES

The Red and Green Tomato Salsas (see pages 2 and 3) would be excellent accompaniments to these delicious tamales.

Serves 4 (3 tamales each)

12 corn husks
   Hot water
12 ounces skinless, boneless chicken breast
   Water
   Vegetable cooking spray
1 medium poblano chili, seeds and veins discarded, chopped
1 medium onion, chopped
1 large tomato, chopped
½ teaspoon minced jalapeño chili
2 cloves garlic, minced
2 tablespoons finely chopped cilantro
¾–1 teaspoon ground cumin
   Salt and pepper, to taste
   Tamale Dough (see preceding recipe)

1. Soak corn husks in hot water until softened, about 1 hour; drain well on paper toweling.
2. Cover chicken with water in small saucepan; heat to boiling. Reduce heat and simmer, covered, until chicken is tender and no longer pink

in the center, 8 to 10 minutes. Drain, reserving ½ cup cooking liquid. Cool chicken slightly; shred into small pieces.

3. Spray medium skillet with cooking spray; heat over medium heat until hot. Saute poblano chili, onion, tomato, jalapeño, and garlic until tender, about 5 minutes. Stir in chicken, cilantro, and cumin and season to taste with salt and pepper. Stir in Tamale Dough and ½ cup reserved cooking liquid.

4. Spoon about ¼ cup of tamale mixture onto center of each corn husk; fold sides of husks over filling. Tie ends of tamales with string, making "bundles."

5. Place tamales on steamer rack in saucepan with 2 inches of water. Steam, covered, 2 hours, adding more water to saucepan if necessary. Serve warm. Makes 12 tamales.

Nutritional Data

PER SERVING		EXCHANGES	
Calories:	285	Milk:	0.0
% Calories from fat:	24	Vegetable:	1.5
Fat (gm):	7.8	Fruit:	0.0
Sat. fat (gm):	1.6	Bread:	1.5
Cholesterol (mg):	51.7	Meat:	2.0
Sodium (gm):	321	Fat:	0.5
Protein (gm):	24.4		
Carbohydrate (gm):	30.2		

BEEF AND PINTO BEAN TAMALES

Tamales can be tied in "bundles," as in the two preceding recipes, or in "envelopes," as in this recipe.

Serves 4 (3 tamales each)

12 corn husks
　Hot water
12 ounces boneless beef eye of round steak, cut
　into l-inch pieces
　Water
　Vegetable cooking spray
1 medium onion, chopped
3 cloves garlic, minced

³/₄ teaspoon dried marjoram leaves
¹/₄ teaspoon ground allspice
¹/₈–¹/₄ teaspoon cayenne pepper
¹/₂ can (15 ounces) pinto beans, rinsed, drained,
    coarsely mashed
    Salt, to taste
    Tamale Dough (see p. 36)

1. Soak corn husks in hot water until softened, about 1 hour; drain well on paper toweling.

2. Cover beef with water in small saucepan; heat to boiling. Reduce heat and simmer, covered, until beef is tender, 15 to 20 minutes. Drain, reserving ¹/₂ cup cooking liquid. Cool beef slightly; shred into small pieces.

3. Spray medium skillet with cooking spray; heat over medium heat until hot. Saute onion, garlic, marjoram, allspice, and pepper until onion is tender, about 5 minutes. Stir in beans and beef and cook 2 to 3 minutes; season to taste with salt. Mix in Tamale Dough and ¹/₂ cup reserved cooking liquid.

4. Spoon about ¹/₄ cup of tamale mixture onto center of each corn husk. Fold sides of husks over filling; fold tops and bottoms of husks toward center and tie in the center with string.

5. Place tamales on steamer rack in saucepan with 2 inches of water. Steam, covered, 2 hours, adding more water to saucepan if necessary. Serve warm. Makes 12 tamales.

Nutritional Data

PER SERVING		EXCHANGES	
Calories:	306	Milk:	0.0
% Calories from fat:	25	Vegetable:	1.0
Fat (gm):	8.5	Fruit:	0.0
Sat. fat (gm):	2	Bread:	2.0
Cholesterol (mg):	41	Meat:	2.0
Sodium (gm):	492	Fat:	0.5
Protein (gm):	23.7		
Carbohydrate (gm):	35.5		

4
ENCHILADAS, TACOS, AND TORTILLA DISHES

Chicken Fajitas

Beef and Roasted Pepper Fajitas

Roasted Vegetable Fajitas

Black Bean and Beef Burritos

Chicken Burritos with Poblano Chili Sauce

Shrimp and Crab Enchiladas with Pasilla Chili Sauce

Chicken Enchiladas Mole

Beef Enchiladas

Chicken Flautas with Tomatillo Sauce

Tacos with Chorizo and Potatoes

Tacos Picadillo

Shrimp Tostados

Chiliquiles

Enchilada Stack

CHICKEN FAJITAS

*Fajitas are an American interpretation of soft tacos.
If grilling fajita ingredients, leave chicken breasts whole
and cut peppers in half, then slice before serving.*

Serves 4 (2 fajitas each)

12 ounces skinless, boneless chicken breast, cut
    into 1½ x ½-inch pieces
    Fajita Marinade (recipe follows)
    Vegetable cooking spray
1 medium red pepper, sliced
1 medium onion, sliced
1 can (15 ounces) black beans, rinsed, drained
1 teaspoon ground cumin
½ teaspoon dried marjoram leaves
    Salt and pepper, to taste
8 flour, or corn, tortillas, warm
2 tablespoons finely chopped cilantro
1 cup Red Tomato Salsa (see p. 2)
½ cup fat-free sour cream

1. Place chicken in shallow glass baking dish; brush Fajita Marinade on chicken. Refrigerate, covered, 1 to 2 hours.

2. Spray large skillet with cooking spray; heat over medium heat until hot. Cook chicken over medium heat until browned and no longer pink in the center, 5 to 8 minutes; move chicken to side of pan. Add pepper and onion; cook over medium heat until tender, about 5 minutes. Add black beans; cook until hot, 2 to 3 minutes. Sprinkle chicken and vegetables with cumin and marjoram; season to taste with salt and pepper.

3. Spoon chicken and vegetable mixture onto tortillas; sprinkle with cilantro, top with Red Tomato Salsa and sour cream, and roll up.

Fajita Marinade

3 tablespoons lime juice
2 cloves garlic, minced
¾ teaspoon dried oregano leaves
¼ teaspoon ground allspice
¼ teaspoon black pepper

1. Mix all ingredients. Makes about 3 tablespoons.

Nutritional Data

PER SERVING		EXCHANGES	
Calories:	424	Milk:	0.0
% Calories from fat:	14	Vegetable:	2.0
Fat (gm):	7.3	Fruit:	0.0
Sat. fat (gm):	1.2	Bread:	3.0
Cholesterol (mg):	51.7	Meat:	2.0
Sodium (gm):	645	Fat:	0.0
Protein (gm):	35.9		
Carbohydrate (gm):	61.7		

BEEF AND ROASTED PEPPER FAJITAS

*The meat in fajitas is normally marinated in lime juice.
In this recipe the lime is not used because the meat is
cooked with the flavorful pasilla chili (see Ingredients).*

Serves 4 (2 fajitas each)

Vegetable cooking spray
1 large red bell pepper
1 large green bell pepper
1 large yellow bell pepper
½–1 teaspoon ground cumin
¼ teaspoon ground cloves
1 dried pasilla chili, stem, seeds, and veins
 discarded
 Hot water
1 pound boneless beef eye of round steak, cut
 into thin strips
3 cloves garlic, minced
¼ small jalapeño chili, seeds and veins discarded,
 minced
 Salt, to taste
8 flour, or corn, tortillas, warm
2 tablespoons finely chopped cilantro
½ cup fat-free sour cream

1. Spray aluminum foil-lined jellyroll pan with cooking spray. Cut peppers
into ¾-inch pieces; arrange on pan and spray with cooking spray. Bake

at 425 degrees until tender and browned, 20 to 25 minutes. Place peppers in bowl; toss with cumin and cloves.

2. Cover pasilla chili with hot water in small bowl; let stand until softened, about 15 minutes. Drain and chop.

3. Spray large skillet with cooking spray; heat over medium heat until hot. Cook beef, garlic, jalapeño, and pasilla chilies over medium heat until beef is desired doneness, about 5 minutes for medium. Season to taste with salt.

4. Spoon beef mixture onto tortillas; sprinkle with cilantro, top with sour cream, and roll up.

Nutritional Data

PER SERVING		EXCHANGES	
Calories:	365	Milk:	0.0
% Calories from fat:	19	Vegetable:	2.0
Fat (gm):	7.8	Fruit:	0.0
Sat. fat (gm):	1.9	Bread:	2.0
Cholesterol (mg):	54.7	Meat:	3.0
Sodium (gm):	355	Fat:	0.0
Protein (gm):	28.9		
Carbohydrate (gm):	45		

ROASTED VEGETABLE FAJITAS

A colorful and flavorful vegetarian entree, although chicken breast or lean beef or pork can be added if you like. The vegetables can be grilled over mesquite chips for a smoky accent. Cut the vegetables in large enough pieces so they don't fall through the grill rack!

Serves 4 (2 fajitas each)

Vegetable cooking spray

2 medium red bell peppers, cut into 3/4-inch strips

2 medium poblano, or green bell peppers, cut into 3/4-inch strips

2 medium onions, cut into wedges

2 medium carrots, cut into 1/2-inch slices

1 large tomato, cut into wedges

1 medium zucchini, cut into 1-inch pieces
1 large chayote squash, unpeeled, seeded, cut
   into 1-inch pieces
8 ounces large mushrooms, cut into halves
2 teaspoons ground cumin
2 teaspoons dried oregano leaves
  Fajita Dressing (recipe follows)
  Salt and pepper, to taste
8 flour, or corn, tortillas, warm

1. Line large jellyroll pan with aluminum foil; spray with cooking spray. Arrange vegetables in pan; spray generously with cooking spray and sprinkle with cumin and oregano.

2. Bake vegetables at 425 degrees until tender and browned, 30 to 40 minutes. Spoon vegetables into serving bowl; drizzle with Fajita Dressing and toss. Season to taste with salt and pepper.

3. Spoon about 1/3 cup of vegetable mixture onto tortillas and roll up.

Fajita Dressing

2 tablespoons olive oil
1 tablespoon lime juice
2–3 teaspoons cider vinegar
2–3 cloves garlic, minced

1. Mix all ingredients. Makes about 1/4 cup.

Nutritional Data

PER SERVING		EXCHANGES	
Calories:	330	Milk:	0.0
% Calories from fat:	30	Vegetable:	4.0
Fat (gm):	11.5	Fruit:	0.0
Sat. fat (gm):	1.6	Bread:	2.0
Cholesterol (mg):	0	Meat:	0.0
Sodium (gm):	264	Fat:	2.0
Protein (gm):	8.8		
Carbohydrate (gm):	51.7		

BLACK BEAN AND BEEF BURRITOS

Another favorite that's a Tex-Mex adaptation of Mexican cooking. The large lo-inch flour tortillas are sometimes called "burritos" on the package. Eight small tortillas can be substituted for the larger size.

Serves 4

Vegetable cooking spray
1 medium poblano chili, seeds and veins discarded, chopped
1 small onion, chopped
1 clove garlic, minced
1 bay leaf, crumbled
1 can (15 ounces) black beans, rinsed, drained
1 can (8 ounces) no-salt-added tomato sauce
Salt and pepper, to taste
Beef Filling (recipe follows)
4 large flour tortillas (10-inch)
½ cup (2 ounces) shredded fat-free Cheddar cheese
½ cup fat-free sour cream
2 tablespoons finely chopped cilantro

1. Spray large skillet with cooking spray; heat over medium heat until hot. Saute poblano chili, onion, garlic, and bay leaf until onion is tender, about 5 minutes. Add beans and tomato sauce; heat until hot. Season to taste with salt and pepper.

2. Spoon bean mixture and Beef Filling along centers of tortillas; top with cheese, sour cream, and cilantro. Roll up; fold one end up to prevent leaking.

Beef Filling

12-16 ounces boneless beef eye of round steak
Water
Vegetable cooking spray
2 medium tomatoes, coarsely chopped
½ teaspoon ground cinnamon
Salt and pepper, to taste

1.   Cut beef into 2-inch cubes and place in saucepan with 2 inches of water; heat to boiling. Reduce heat and simmer, covered, until beef is tender, 15 to 20 minutes; drain. Cool slightly; shred finely.

2.   Spray medium skillet with cooking spray; heat over medium heat until hot. Cook beef until beginning to brown, 3 to 4 minutes. Add tomatoes and cinnamon; cook until tomatoes are wilted. Season to taste with salt and pepper. Makes about 2 cups.

Nutritional Data

PER SERVING		EXCHANGES	
Calories:	379	Milk:	0.0
% Calories from fat:	14	Vegetable:	2.0
Fat (gm):	6.5	Fruit:	0.0
Sat. fat (gm):	1.4	Bread:	2.5
Cholesterol (mg):	43.6	Meat:	2.5
Sodium (gm):	677	Fat:	0.0
Protein (gm):	35.5		
Carbohydrate (gm):	51.8		

CHICKEN BURRITOS WITH POBLANO CHILI SAUCE

Brushed with sauce and cooked twice for extra flavor, these burritos are a beautiful adobe red color.

Serves 4

12–16 ounces skinless, boneless chicken breast, cut into l-inch cubes
        Water
        Salt and pepper, to taste
    3   arbol chilies, stems, seeds, and veins discarded
        Hot water
        Vegetable cooking spray
    1   small onion, finely chopped
    3   cloves garlic, minced
    2   tablespoons finely chopped cilantro
    1   teaspoon dried marjoram leaves
    1   teaspoon dried oregano leaves
    1   can (15 ounces) pinto beans, rinsed, drained
    1/4 teaspoon cayenne pepper

Salt, to taste
4 large flour tortillas (10 inch)
Poblano Chili Sauce (see p. 115)
½ cup fat-free sour cream
Medium or hot prepared salsa, to taste

1. Cover chicken with water in small saucepan; heat to boiling. Reduce heat and simmer, covered, until chicken is tender and no longer pink in the center, 8 to 10 minutes. Drain, reserving ¼ cup cooking liquid. Cool chicken slightly; shred into small pieces. Season lightly with salt and pepper to taste.

2. Cover arbol chilies with hot water in small bowl; let stand until softened, 10 to 15 minutes. Drain; chop finely.

3. Spray medium skillet with cooking spray; heat over medium heat until hot. Saute onion, garlic, and herbs until onion is tender, 3 to 4 minutes. Add beans, ¼ cup reserved cooking liquid, and arbol chilies to skillet; mash coarsely with fork. Cook over medium heat until hot; season with cayenne pepper and salt to taste.

4. Spoon bean mixture and chicken along centers of tortillas; top each with ¼ cup Poblano Chili Sauce. Fold sides of tortillas in, overlapping over filling; fold ends in, overlapping to make a square "package"; secure with toothpicks.

5. Spray large skillet with cooking spray; heat over medium heat until hot. Cook burritos until browned on all sides, brushing with remaining Poblano Chili Sauce. Serve hot with sour cream and salsa.

Nutritional Data

PER SERVING		EXCHANGES	
Calories:	385	Milk:	0.0
% Calories from fat:	14	Vegetable:	2.0
Fat (gm):	6.1	Fruit:	0.0
Sat. fat (gm):	1.1	Bread:	3.0
Cholesterol (mg):	51.7	Meat:	2.0
Sodium (gm):	661	Fat:	0.0
Protein (gm):	33.1		
Carbohydrate (gm):	52.6		

SHRIMP AND CRAB ENCHILADAS WITH PASILLA CHILI SAUCE

The rich Pasilla Chili Sauce is creamy in texture, slightly smoky in flavor. It is also excellent served with Chicken and Cheese Rellenos (see p. 65) or with grilled chicken breast or lean pork.

Serves 4 (2 enchiladas each)

- 8 ounces peeled, deveined shrimp, cooked, coarsely chopped
- 4 ounces Alaskan king crab, or peeled, deveined shrimp
  Pasilla Chili Sauce (recipe follows)
- 8 flour tortillas
- 1/2 cup (2 ounces) shredded fat-free Cheddar cheese
- 1/4 cup finely chopped cilantro

1. Combine shrimp, crab, and 3/4 cup Pasilla Chili Sauce. Spoon equal portions on tortillas and roll up. Place tortillas, seam sides down, in lightly greased glass baking dish, 11 x 7 inches. Spoon remaining Pasilla Chili Sauce over enchiladas; sprinkle with cheese.

2. Bake enchiladas, uncovered, at 350 degrees until hot through, about 20 minutes. Sprinkle with cilantro.

Pasilla Chili Sauce

- Vegetable cooking spray
- 3 pasilla chilies
- 2 medium tomatoes, coarsely chopped
- 1 small onion, coarsely chopped
- 1/2 teaspoon sugar
- 1 cup fat-free sour cream
- Salt and pepper, to taste

1. Spray small skillet with cooking spray; heat over medium heat until hot. Cook chilies over medium heat until soft; remove and discard stems, seeds, and veins. Process chilies, tomatoes, onion, and sugar in blender until smooth.

2. Spray large skillet with cooking spray; heat over medium heat until hot. Cook chili mixture over medium heat, stirring occasionally, until thickened, about 5 minutes. Reduce heat to low; stir in sour cream and cook until hot through. Season to taste with salt and pepper. Makes about 2 cups.

Nutritional Data

PER SERVING		EXCHANGES	
Calories:	318	Milk:	0.0
% Calories from fat:	13	Vegetable:	0.5
Fat (gm):	4.5	Fruit:	0.0
Sat. fat (gm):	0.7	Bread:	2.0
Cholesterol (mg):	101.9	Meat:	3.0
Sodium (gm):	722	Fat:	0.0
Protein (gm):	28.3		
Carbohydrate (gm):	41.2		

CHICKEN ENCHILADAS MOLE

For variation, the enchiladas can also be baked with Tomatillo Sauce or Jalapeño con Queso Sauce (see pages 118 and 117). Serve with Jicama Salad (see p. 109) for fresh-flavor contrast.

Serves 4 (2 enchiladas each)

8 corn, or flour, tortillas
1 cup Enchilada Sauce (see p. 116), or prepared salsa
1 pound boneless, skinless chicken breast, cooked, shredded
½ cup (2 ounces) shredded fat-free Cheddar cheese
½ cup sliced green onions and tops
4–8 tablespoons fat-free sour cream
¼ cup finely chopped cilantro
Mole Sauce (see p. 119)

1. Dip tortillas in Enchilada Sauce to coat lightly. Spoon chicken along centers of tortillas; top with cheese, green onions, sour cream, and cilantro. Roll up and place, seam sides down, in large baking pan. Spoon Mole Sauce over enchiladas.

2. Bake, loosely covered, at 350 degrees until enchiladas are hot through, 20 to 30 minutes.

Nutritional Data

PER SERVING		EXCHANGES	
Calories:	401	Milk:	0.0
% Calories from fat:	19	Vegetable:	2.0
Fat (gm):	8.5	Fruit:	0.0
Sat. fat (gm):	1.5	Bread:	2.0
Cholesterol (mg):	71.5	Meat:	4.0
Sodium (gm):	294	Fat:	0.0
Protein (gm):	39.3		
Carbohydrate (gm):	44.2		

BEEF ENCHILADAS

◆

Vary these healthful enchiladas by substituting shredded chicken or pork tenderloin for the beef.

Serves 6 (2 enchiladas each)

Vegetable cooking spray
2 cups chopped zucchini
1½ cups chopped tomato
¾ cup chopped carrots
¼ cup chopped poblano chili, or green bell pepper
¼ cup thinly sliced green onions and tops
4 cloves garlic, minced
1 teaspoon minced serrano, or jalapeño, chili
1 teaspoon dried oregano leaves
1–2 teaspoons ground cumin
1½ pounds boneless beef eye of round, cooked, shredded
Salt and pepper, to taste
12 corn, or flour, tortillas
Enchilada Sauce (see p. 116)
¾ cup (3 ounces) shredded fat-free Cheddar cheese
3 tablespoons finely chopped cilantro

1. Spray large skillet with cooking spray; heat over medium heat until hot. Saute vegetables and herbs until vegetables are tender, about 10

minutes. Add beef; cook over medium heat until no excess juices remain, 5 to 8 minutes. Season to taste with salt and pepper.

2. Dip tortillas in Enchilada Sauce to coat lightly and fill each with about ⅓ cup of beef mixture. Roll up and place, seam sides down, in large baking pan. Spoon remaining Enchilada Sauce over enchiladas; sprinkle with cheese.

3. Bake enchiladas, uncovered, at 350 degrees, 15 to 20 minutes. Sprinkle with cilantro.

Nutritional Data

PER SERVING		EXCHANGES	
Calories:	304	Milk:	0.0
% Calories from fat:	16	Vegetable:	2.0
Fat (gm):	5.5	Fruit:	0.0
Sat. fat (gm):	1.5	Bread:	1.5
Cholesterol (mg):	57.2	Meat:	3.0
Sodium (gm):	244	Fat:	0.0
Protein (gm):	30.2		
Carbohydrate (gm):	34.8		

CHICKEN FLAUTAS WITH TOMATILLO SAUCE

————◆————

Flautas are usually deep-fried; these are sauteed to achieve the same crispness.

Serves 4 (2 flautas each)

Vegetable cooking spray
1 cup chopped tomato
¼ cup chopped onion
2–4 tablespoons finely chopped poblano chili
½ teaspoon ground cumin
¼ teaspoon dried thyme leaves
1 pound skinless, boneless chicken breast, cooked, shredded
2 tablespoons finely chopped cilantro
Salt and pepper, to taste
8 flour, or corn, tortillas
1 cup Tomatillo Sauce (see p. 118)

4 tablespoons crumbled Mexican white cheese,
  or farmer's cheese
¼ cup fat-free sour cream
  Cilantro sprigs, as garnish

1. Spray large skillet with cooking spray; heat over medium heat until
   hot. Saute tomato, onion, poblano chili, cumin, and thyme until onion
   is tender, about 5 minutes. Add chicken and cilantro; cook 2 to 3
   minutes more. Season to taste with salt and pepper.

2. Spoon about ⅓ cup chicken mixture on each tortilla; roll up and fasten
   with toothpicks. Spray large skillet generously with cooking spray;
   heat over medium heat until hot. Cook flautas over medium to
   medium-high heat until browned on all sides, spraying with cooking
   spray if needed.

3. Arrange flautas on plates; spoon Tomatillo Sauce over. Sprinkle with
   cheese; top with dollops of sour cream. Garnish with cilantro.

Nutritional Data

PER SERVING		EXCHANGES	
Calories:	388	Milk:	0.0
% Calories from fat:	23	Vegetable:	2.0
Fat (gm):	9.8	Fruit:	0.0
Sat. fat (gm):	1.4	Bread:	2.0
Cholesterol (mg):	75.7	Meat:	3.5
Sodium (gm):	361	Fat:	0.0
Protein (gm):	34		
Carbohydrate (gm):	40.6		

TACOS WITH CHORIZO AND POTATOES

◆

In many parts of Mexico, fried tacos are made by pan-sauteing folded, filled tortillas—a delectable alternative to the crisp taco shells we are accustomed to! Our low-fat version uses vegetable cooking spray in place of traditional lard for sauteing.

Serves 4 (2 tacos each)

Vegetable cooking spray
Chorizo (see p. 70)
1 cup chopped onion
1 cup cubed cooked potato
1 cup (4 ounces) shredded fat-free Cheddar cheese
2 tablespoons finely chopped cilantro
Salt and pepper, to taste
8 corn, or flour, tortillas
½ cup Tomatillo Sauce, or Jalapeño con Queso Sauce (see pages 118 and117)
¼ cup fat-free sour cream

1. Spray large skillet with cooking spray; heat over medium heat until hot. Cook Chorizo over medium heat 2 to 3 minutes. Add onion and potato and cook until onion is tender and Chorizo cooked, about 5 minutes. Remove from heat; stir in cheese and cilantro. Season to taste with salt and pepper.

2. Heat tortillas in skillet or microwave oven until softened. Spoon about ½ cup Chorizo mixture on each tortilla and fold in half to make tacos. Spray large skillet with cooking spray; heat over medium heat until hot. Saute tacos until lightly browned, 1 to 2 minutes on each side. Serve with Tomatillo Sauce and sour cream.

Nutritional Data

PER SERVING		EXCHANGES	
Calories:	358	Milk:	0.0
% Calories from fat:	13	Vegetable:	2.0
Fat (gm):	5.1	Fruit:	0.0
Sat. fat (gm):	1.3	Bread:	2.0
Cholesterol (mg):	54.1	Meat:	3.0
Sodium (gm):	606	Fat:	0.0
Protein (gm):	32.9		
Carbohydrate (gm):	46.6		

TACOS PICADILLO

Chicken breast or lean beef can be substituted for the pork. Serve these tacos with Red or Green Tomato Salsa (see pages 2 and 3).

Serves 6 (2 tacos each)

1½ pounds boneless pork tenderloin, cut into
   1-inch cubes
   Water
   Vegetable cooking spray
½ cup chopped onion
4 cloves garlic, minced
1 small jalapeño chili, seeds and veins discarded,
   minced
2 medium tomatoes, chopped
¼ cup dark raisins
2 tablespoons slivered almonds, toasted
1–2 tablespoons cider vinegar
1½–2 teaspoons ground cinnamon
½ teaspoon ground cloves
½ teaspoon dried oregano leaves
¼ teaspoon ground allspice
   Salt and pepper, to taste
12 flour, or corn, tortillas

1. Cover pork with water in medium saucepan; heat to boiling. Reduce heat and simmer, covered, until pork is tender, about 10 minutes. Drain; cool pork slightly and shred into small pieces.

2. Spray medium skillet with cooking spray; heat over medium heat until hot. Saute onion, garlic, and jalapeño chili until tender, about 5 minutes. Add pork, tomatoes, raisins, almonds, vinegar, cinnamon,

cloves, oregano, and allspice. Cook over medium heat, stirring occasionally, until pork is hot through and mixture is dry, about 5 minutes. Season to taste with salt and pepper.

3. Spoon about ⅓ cup of mixture on each tortilla and fold in half to make tacos. Spray large skillet with cooking spray; heat over medium heat until hot. Saute tacos until lightly browned, 1 to 2 minutes on each side.

Nutritional Data

PER SERVING		EXCHANGES	
Calories:	351	Milk:	0.0
% Calories from fat:	23	Vegetable:	1.5
Fat (gm):	9.1	Fruit:	0.0
Sat. fat (gm):	2.1	Bread:	2.0
Cholesterol (mg):	65.4	Meat:	3.0
Sodium (gm):	302	Fat:	0.0
Protein (gm):	29.1		
Carbohydrate (gm):	37.8		

SHRIMP TOSTADOS

◆

A perfect brunch or lunch entree, South-of-the-Border style! Serve with Zucchini from Puebla, Yellow Salsa Rice, or Refried Beans (see pages 103, 98, and 102).

Serves 4

Vegetable cooking spray
4 corn tortillas
16 ounces peeled, deveined medium shrimp
1 small onion, chopped
½ serrano chili, seeds and veins discarded, finely chopped
1 cup Chili Tomato Sauce (see p. 114), warm
2 cups chopped romaine lettuce
1 medium tomato, chopped
¼ cup crumbled Mexican white cheese, or farmer's cheese
½ Guacamole recipe (see p. 8)

1. Spray medium skillet with cooking spray; heat over medium heat until hot. Cook tortillas until crisp and browned, about 1 minute on each side. Place tortillas on serving plates.

2. Reserve 4 whole shrimp for garnish; cut remaining shrimp into halves or thirds. Spray medium saucepan with cooking spray; heat over medium heat until hot. Cook whole and cut shrimp, onion, and serrano chili until shrimp are cooked and pink, 3 to 5 minutes. Reserve the 4 whole shrimp. Combine remaining shrimp mixture with Chili Tomato Sauce.

3. Top tortillas with chopped lettuce and tomato; spoon shrimp mixture over. Sprinkle with crumbled cheese; top each with a large dollop of Guacamole and a whole shrimp.

Nutritional Data

PER SERVING		EXCHANGES	
Calories:	245	Milk:	0.0
% Calories from fat:	21	Vegetable:	2.0
Fat (gm):	5.8	Fruit:	0.0
Sat. fat (gm):	0.7	Bread:	1.0
Cholesterol (mg):	181.7	Meat:	1.5
Sodium (gm):	332	Fat:	0.0
Protein (gm):	24.5		
Carbohydrate (gm):	24		

CHILIQUILES

Leftovers, Mexican-style! Chiliquiles is a family-style casserole dish usually made with day-old tortillas and leftover cooked meats. Vary this casserole with ingredients you have on hand!

Serves 8

8 corn, or flour, tortillas
   Vegetable cooking spray
1 medium green bell pepper, thinly sliced
1/2 teaspoon minced jalapeño chili pepper
1/4 teaspoon cayenne pepper
   Enchilada Sauce (see p. 116)
1 1/2 cups cooked black beans, or 1 can (15 ounces) black beans, rinsed, drained
1 cup frozen thawed whole kernel corn, or fresh corn
12–16 ounces cooked, skinless, shredded chicken breast
1 large tomato, thinly sliced

Jalapeño con Queso Sauce (see p. 117)
Medium or hot salsa, to taste

1. Spray both sides of tortillas lightly with cooking spray; cook in small skillet over medium-high heat to brown lightly, 30 to 60 seconds per side. Cool slightly; cut into ½-inch strips.

2. Spray small skillet with cooking spray; heat over medium heat until hot. Saute peppers until tender, 2 to 3 minutes; sprinkle with cayenne pepper. Stir in Enchilada Sauce; heat until hot.

3. Arrange ⅓ of the tortilla strips in bottom of 2-quart casserole. Top with ½ cup black beans, ⅓ cup corn, ⅓ of the chicken, ⅓ of the tomato slices, and ⅔ cup Jalapeño con Queso Sauce. Repeat layers 2 times.

4. Bake casserole, uncovered, at 350 degrees until hot through, 25 to 30 minutes. Serve hot with salsa.

Nutritional Data

PER SERVING		EXCHANGES	
Calories:	292	Milk:	0.0
% Calories from fat:	16	Vegetable:	1.0
Fat (gm):	5.4	Fruit:	0.0
Sat. fat (gm):	2.6	Bread:	1.5
Cholesterol (mg):	46.1	Meat:	3.0
Sodium (gm):	634	Fat:	0.0
Protein (gm):	30.1		
Carbohydrate (gm):	32.5		

ENCHILADA STACK

A quick and easy casserole. Corn tortillas are layered with pork, beans, and chilies mixture and Enchilada Sauce, then baked until hot—a Mexican fiesta of flavors, perfect for brunch!

Serves 4

12 ounces boneless pork tenderloin, cut into 1-inch slices
Water
Vegetable cooking spray
1 medium onion, chopped
1 can (15 ounces) pinto beans, rinsed, drained
1 medium tomato, chopped
1 can (4 ounces) chopped green chilies, drained

1½ teaspoons ground cumin
¼ teaspoon pepper
5 corn tortillas
Enchilada Sauce (see p. 116)
½ cup (2 ounces) shredded reduced-fat Cheddar
cheese
⅓ cup fat-free sour cream

1. Place pork tenderloin in saucepan with 2 inches of water; heat to boiling. Reduce heat and simmer, covered, until pork is tender, about 10 minutes. Drain. Cool slightly and shred finely.

2. Spray medium skillet with cooking spray; heat over medium heat until hot. Saute onion until tender, 3 to 4 minutes. Add shredded pork, beans, tomato, chilies, cumin, and pepper; cook over medium heat until hot, 3 to 4 minutes.

3. Place 1 tortilla in bottom of 1-quart soufflé dish or casserole; spoon ¼ of the bean mixture over tortilla. Spoon ⅓ cup Enchilada Sauce over. Repeat layers three times, ending with a tortilla and remaining ⅔ cup of Enchilada Sauce. Sprinkle with cheese.

4. Bake, covered, at 350 degrees until hot through, 25 to 30 minutes. Let stand 5 minutes; cut into 4 wedges. Serve with sour cream.

Nutritional Data

PER SERVING		EXCHANGES	
Calories:	379	Milk:	0.0
% Calories from fat:	16	Vegetable:	2.0
Fat (gm):	7.2	Fruit:	0.0
Sat. fat (gm):	2.2	Bread:	2.5
Cholesterol (mg):	56.7	Meat:	2.5
Sodium (gm):	793	Fat:	0.0
Protein (gm):	33.1		
Carbohydrate (gm):	49.4		

5
MEAT AND POULTRY

Lime Chicken and Onions

Orange Chicken and Vegetables

Chicken Mole

Chicken and Cheese Rellenos

Chicken and Pork Stew with Fruit

Pork Tenderloin with Green Peanut Sauce

Savory Stewed Pork and Chorizo

Chorizo

Meatballs in Tomato Chili Sauce

Beef and Ancho Chili Stew

Beef Steaks with Tomatillo and Avocado Sauce

Mexican Hash

Chili con Carne

LIME CHICKEN AND ONIONS

The chicken is superb grilled with mesquite charcoal. Cook over medium-hot coals, basting frequently with Lime Sauce, until golden and no longer pink in the center, about 15 minutes.

Serves 4

Vegetable cooking spray
4 skinless, boneless chicken breast halves
(about 4 ounces each)
Lime Sauce (recipe follows)
3 cups sliced onions
Salt and pepper, to taste
3 cups cooked rice, warm
Finely chopped cilantro, as garnish

1. Spray large skillet generously with cooking spray. Cook chicken over medium heat until browned on both sides and no longer pink in the center, 10 to 15 minutes, basting frequently with Lime Sauce.

2. Move chicken to side of skillet. Add onions to skillet; cook over medium heat, basting frequently with Lime Sauce, until tender and lightly browned, 5 to 8 minutes. Season chicken and onions to taste with salt and pepper.

3. Arrange chicken, onions, and rice on serving plates; sprinkle generously with cilantro. Serve with any remaining Lime Sauce.

Lime Sauce

1 cup water
$2/3$ cup lime juice
$1/2$ cup sugar
1 clove garlic, minced
$1/2$ teaspoon chili powder
2 tablespoons cornstarch
$1/4$ cup lemon juice

1. Heat water, lime juice, sugar, garlic, and chili powder in small saucepan to boiling. Mix cornstarch and lemon juice; stir into boiling mixture. Boil, stirring constantly, until thickened, about 1 minute. Use immediately, or cool to room temperature and refrigerate. Makes about 2 cups.

Nutritional Data

PER SERVING		EXCHANGES	
Calories:	462	Milk:	0.0
% Calories from fat:	7	Vegetable:	2.0
Fat (gm):	3.5	Fruit:	0.0
Sat. fat (gm):	1	Bread:	4.0
Cholesterol (mg):	69	Meat:	2.5
Sodium (gm):	69	Fat:	0.0
Protein (gm):	30.2		
Carbohydrate (gm):	77.8		

ORANGE CHICKEN AND VEGETABLES

Oranges are grown in many parts of Mexico and are a popular ingredient in cooking. Both orange juice and rind are used to accent this family-style dish.

Serves 6

Vegetable cooking spray
6 skinless, boneless chicken breast halves (about 1½ pounds)
1 large onion, sliced
2 cloves garlic, chopped
1 tablespoon flour
3 medium tomatoes, chopped
½ teaspoon dried marjoram leaves
¼ teaspoon dried thyme leaves
1 cinnamon stick, 1-inch piece
1½ cups orange juice
2 teaspoons grated orange rind
3 large carrots, cut into 1-inch pieces
3 medium potatoes, unpeeled, cubed
Salt and pepper, to taste

1. Spray large skillet with cooking spray; heat over medium heat until hot. Cook chicken over medium heat until browned, about 5 minutes on each side. Arrange chicken in glass baking dish, 12 x 9 inches.

2. Spray skillet with cooking spray again; heat over medium heat until hot. Saute onion and garlic until tender, 5 to 8 minutes. Stir in flour;

cook over medium heat l to 2 minutes. Add tomatoes, marjoram, thyme, and cinnamon; saute l to 2 minutes.

3. Add orange juice and rind to skillet; heat to boiling. Reduce heat and simmer, uncovered, 5 minutes. Arrange carrots and potatoes around chicken in casserole; pour orange juice mixture over. Bake, covered, at 350 degrees until chicken is tender, about 30 minutes. Season to taste with salt and pepper.

Nutritional Data

PER SERVING		EXCHANGES	
Calories:	318	Milk:	0.0
% Calories from fat:	10	Vegetable:	2.0
Fat (gm):	3.5	Fruit:	0.5
Sat. fat (gm):	0.9	Bread:	1.5
Cholesterol (mg):	69	Meat:	2.5
Sodium (gm):	87	Fat:	0.0
Protein (gm):	29.4		
Carbohydrate (gm):	42.4		

CHICKEN MOLE

Serve this traditional dish with Corn Pudding, Potatoes with Chilies, Refried Beans, or Orange Cilantro Rice (see pp. 107, 104, 102, and 99).

Serves 6

Vegetable cooking spray
6–8 skinless chicken breasts (about 6 ounces each)
Mole Sauce (see p. 119)
3 tablespoons finely chopped cilantro

1. Spray large skillet with cooking spray; heat over medium heat until hot. Cook chicken breasts over medium heat until browned, 8 to l0 minutes. Arrange in large baking pan.

2. Spoon Mole Sauce over chicken. Bake, loosely covered, at 350 degrees until chicken is tender and no longer pink in the center, about 30 minutes. Arrange chicken on serving platter; sprinkle with cilantro.

Nutritional Data

PER SERVING		EXCHANGES	
Calories:	211	Milk:	0.0
% Calories from fat:	25	Vegetable:	2.0
Fat (gm):	5.8	Fruit:	0.0
Sat. fat (gm):	1.2	Bread:	0.0
Cholesterol (mg):	68.6	Meat:	3.0
Sodium (gm):	87	Fat:	0.0
Protein (gm):	28.6		
Carbohydrate (gm):	11.2		

CHICKEN AND CHEESE RELLENOS

*Any lean meat can be substituted for the chicken. Our
healthy version of chiles rellenos deletes the customary
egg coating and minimizes skillet oil. Choose either sauce: the
Chili Tomato Sauce is more highly spiced; the sour cream Pasilla
Chili Sauce is delicately spiced and slightly smoky.*

Serves 4

     6 large poblano chilies
 2–3 quarts water
        Vegetable cooking spray
     1 medium onion, chopped
     1 carrot, cooked crisp-tender, coarsely chopped
     1 clove garlic, chopped
    16 ounces boneless, skinless chicken breast,
          cooked, shredded
   1/2 cup frozen, thawed whole kernel corn
   1/2 teaspoon ground cumin
   1/2 teaspoon dried thyme leaves
   1/2 cup (2 ounces) shredded reduced-fat Monterey
          Jack cheese
   1/2 cup (2 ounces) shredded fat-free Cheddar
          cheese
        Salt and pepper, to taste
     1 tablespoon vegetable oil
     1 cup Chili Tomato Sauce, or Pasilla Chili Sauce
          (see pages 114 and 49)

1. Cut stems from tops of chilies; remove and discard seeds and veins. Heat water to boiling in large saucepan; add peppers. Reduce heat and simmer, uncovered, 2 to 3 minutes, until peppers are slightly softened. Drain well and cool; reserve peppers.

2. Coat large skillet with cooking spray; heat over medium heat until hot. Saute onion, carrot, and garlic until tender, 3 to 5 minutes. Add chicken, corn, and herbs; cook over medium heat 1 to 2 minutes. Remove from heat; stir in cheeses. Season to taste with salt and pepper.

3. Stuff peppers with mixture. Heat oil in medium skillet until hot. Saute peppers over medium to medium-high heat until tender and browned on all sides, 6 to 8 minutes. Serve with Chili Tomato Sauce (included in Nutritional Data below) or Pasilla Chili Sauce.

Nutritional Data

PER SERVING		EXCHANGES	
Calories:	323	Milk:	0.0
% Calories from fat:	26	Vegetable:	3.0
Fat (gm):	9.6	Fruit:	0.0
Sat. fat (gm):	2.8	Bread:	0.5
Cholesterol (mg):	81.6	Meat:	4.0
Sodium (gm):	319	Fat:	0.0
Protein (gm):	37.9		
Carbohydrate (gm):	22.6		

CHICKEN AND PORK STEW WITH FRUIT

A luscious stew with flavor accents of tropical fruit, sweet cinnamon, and piquant ancho chili.

Serves 6

Vegetable cooking spray

12 ounces pork tenderloin, cut into 1½-inch cubes

12 ounces skinless, boneless chicken breast, cut into 1½-inch cubes

2 tablespoons slivered almonds

1 tablespoon sesame seed

1 cinnamon stick, 1-inch piece

3 ancho chilies, stems, seeds, and veins
discarded

2 medium tomatoes, cut into 1-inch pieces

1 can (14½ ounces) fat-free, reduced-sodium
chicken broth, divided

1 cup peeled, cubed jicama

1 cup cubed pineapple, or 1 can (8 ounces)
pineapple chunks, drained

1 small ripe plantain, cut into ½-inch pieces
Salt and pepper, to taste

4 cups cooked rice, warm (optional)

1. Spray large skillet with cooking spray; heat over medium heat until
hot. Cook pork and chicken over medium heat until browned, about 5
minutes. Remove from skillet.

2. Add almonds, sesame seed, and cinnamon to skillet. Cook over
medium heat until almonds and sesame seed are toasted, 3 to 4
minutes; transfer mixture to blender container. Add chilies and
tomatoes to skillet and cook over medium heat until tomatoes are soft,
1 to 2 minutes; transfer to blender. Add 1 cup broth to blender and
process until mixture is smooth.

3. Spray medium saucepan with cooking spray; heat over medium heat
until hot. Cook chili mixture over medium heat until slightly
thickened, 4 to 5 minutes. Add meat mixture, remaining broth, jicama,
and fruit; heat to boiling. Reduce heat and simmer, covered, until
meats are tender, about 30 minutes. Season to taste with salt and
pepper. Serve over rice.

Nutritional Data

PER SERVING		EXCHANGES	
Calories:	239	Milk:	0.0
% Calories from fat:	22	Vegetable:	1.0
Fat (gm):	5.9	Fruit:	1.0
Sat. fat (gm):	1.4	Bread:	0.0
Cholesterol (mg):	67.2	Meat:	3.0
Sodium (gm):	81	Fat:	0.0
Protein (gm):	28.1		
Carbohydrate (gm):	19.6		

PORK TENDERLOIN WITH GREEN PEANUT SAUCE

*Although the true Mexican version of Green Peanut Sauce uses
a much larger quantity of peanuts, this lower-fat version is
very flavorful, with a pleasing crunchy texture.*

Serves 6

1 clove garlic, cut in half
  Vegetable cooking spray
1½ pounds pork tenderloin, cut into ¼-inch slices
  Salt and pepper, to taste
1 cup Tomatillo Sauce (see p. 118)
⅓ cup chopped light dry-roasted peanuts
4 cups cooked rice, warm

1. Rub bottom of large skillet with cut sides of garlic. Spray skillet with cooking spray; heat over medium heat until hot. Add pork to skillet and cook over medium to medium-high heat until no longer pink in the center, 3 to 4 minutes on each side. Sprinkle lightly with salt and pepper.

2. Add Tomatillo Sauce to skillet; stir in peanuts and heat until hot. Serve over rice.

Nutritional Data

PER SERVING		EXCHANGES	
Calories:	347	Milk:	0.0
% Calories from fat:	23	Vegetable:	1.0
Fat (gm):	8.9	Fruit:	0.0
Sat. fat (gm):	2	Bread:	2.0
Cholesterol (mg):	65.4	Meat:	3.0
Sodium (gm):	115	Fat:	0.0
Protein (gm):	28.9		
Carbohydrate (gm):	36.6		

SAVORY STEWED PORK AND CHORIZO

A versatile dish, this shredded pork and chorizo "stew" is generally served rolled in a tortilla or used as a topping for tostados. A less tender cut of meat would typically be used, but pork tenderloin keeps this dish skinny.

Serves 6 (about ⅔ cup each)

12 ounces pork tenderloin, cut into 1-inch cubes
Water
Vegetable cooking spray
Chorizo (see p. 70)
1 small onion, sliced
1 clove garlic, minced
2 large tomatoes, chopped
¼ teaspoon dried oregano leaves
¼ teaspoon dried thyme leaves
1 bay leaf
2–3 pickled jalapeño chilies, finely chopped
1 tablespoon pickled jalapeño juice
Salt and pepper, to taste
4 cups cooked rice, warm (optional)

1. Cover pork with water in medium saucepan; heat to boiling. Reduce heat and simmer, covered, until tender, 20 to 30 minutes. Cool and drain, reserving ½ cup broth. Finely shred pork.

2. Spray large skillet with cooking spray; heat over medium heat until hot. Cook Chorizo over medium heat until done; remove from skillet and crumble. Add onion and garlic to skillet; saute 2 to 3 minutes. Add tomatoes and herbs and cook over medium heat 5 minutes, stirring occasionally.

3. Add pork, Chorizo, ½ cup reserved broth, jalapeño chilies, and jalapeño juice to skillet. Cook, uncovered, over medium heat, about 10 minutes, stirring occasionally (mixture should be moist, not dry). Discard bay leaf; season to taste with salt and pepper. Serve over rice, if desired.

Nutritional Data

PER SERVING		EXCHANGES	
Calories:	161	Milk:	0.0
% Calories from fat:	25	Vegetable:	1.0
Fat (gm):	4.4	Fruit:	0.0
Sat. fat (gm):	2.9	Bread:	0.0
Cholesterol (mg):	65.5	Meat:	4.0
Sodium (gm):	300	Fat:	0.0
Protein (gm):	24.3		
Carbohydrate (gm):	5.6		

CHORIZO

*Chorizo is a well-seasoned Mexican sausage made with pork.
The seasonings vary from region to region in Mexico and are
often quite hot and spicy. Paprika gives the sausage its
traditional red color. The sausage patties can be served with
eggs, or the sausage can be cooked and crumbled to serve
in quesadillas, nachos, enchiladas, and so on.*

Serves 4 (1 patty each)

Vegetable cooking spray
¼ teaspoon coriander seed, crushed
¼ teaspoon cumin seed, crushed, or ⅛ teaspoon
  ground cumin
1 dried ancho chili
12 ounces boneless pork tenderloin, all fat
  trimmed, finely chopped or ground
2 cloves garlic, minced
1 tablespoon paprika
½ teaspoon dried oregano leaves
½–¾ teaspoon salt
1 tablespoon cider vinegar
1 tablespoon water

1. Spray small skillet with cooking spray; heat over medium heat until hot. Add coriander and cumin seed; cook over medium heat, stirring frequently, until toasted. Remove from skillet.

2. Add ancho chili to skillet; cook over medium heat until softened, about 1 minute on each side, turning so that chili does not burn. Remove and discard stem, veins, and seeds. Chop chili finely.

3. Combine pork tenderloin and all remaining ingredients in small bowl, mixing thoroughly. Refrigerate, covered, at least 4 hours or overnight for flavors to blend.

4. Spray small skillet with cooking spray; heat over medium heat until hot. Shape pork mixture into 4 patties; cook over medium heat until cooked through, 4 to 5 minutes on each side. (Or, recipe makes 2 cups crumbled sausage.)

Nutritional Data

PER SERVING		EXCHANGES	
Calories:	112	Milk:	0.0
% Calories from fat:	27	Vegetable:	0.0
Fat (gm):	3.3	Fruit:	0.0
Sat. fat (gm):	1.1	Bread:	0.0
Cholesterol (mg):	49.1	Meat:	2.0
Sodium (gm):	308	Fat:	0.0
Protein (gm):	17.9		
Carbohydrate (gm):	2.1		

MEATBALLS IN TOMATO CHILI SAUCE

The meatballs can be made in advance and frozen; thaw before using. The pasilla chilies are picante—use 2 only if you enjoy a truly hot sauce!

Serves 4 (4 meatballs each)

½ pound ground pork tenderloin
½ pound ground beef rib eye steak
2 egg whites
¼ cup dry unseasoned breadcrumbs
½ cup finely chopped zucchini
¼ cup finely chopped onion
2 cloves garlic, minced
1 teaspoon minced jalapeño chili
½ teaspoon dried oregano leaves
¼ teaspoon dried thyme leaves
½ teaspoon salt
⅛ teaspoon pepper
  Vegetable cooking spray

 1–2 pasilla chilies
    1 can (28 ounces) reduced-sodium diced
       tomatoes, undrained
       Salt and pepper, to taste

1. Mix ground pork and beef, egg whites, breadcrumbs, zucchini, onion, garlic, jalapeño chili, oregano, thyme, ½ teaspoon salt, and ⅛ teaspoon pepper. Shape mixture into 16 meatballs.

2. Spray large saucepan with cooking spray; heat over medium heat until hot. Cook pasilla chilies over medium heat until softened; discard stems, seeds, and veins. Process chilies and tomatoes with liquid in blender until smooth.

3. Heat tomato mixture to boiling in large saucepan; add meatballs. Reduce heat and simmer, covered, until meatballs are cooked and no longer pink in the center, about 10 minutes. Season to taste with salt and pepper.

Nutritional Data

PER SERVING		EXCHANGES	
Calories:	240	Milk:	0.0
% Calories from fat:	24	Vegetable:	3.0
Fat (gm):	6.5	Fruit:	0.0
Sat. fat (gm):	2.3	Bread:	0.0
Cholesterol (mg):	60.9	Meat:	3.0
Sodium (gm):	435	Fat:	0.0
Protein (gm):	29.3		
Carbohydrate (gm):	15.9		

BEEF AND ANCHO CHILI STEW

This stew has lots of delicious sauce, so serve with crusty warm rolls or warm tortillas, or serve over Black Beans and Rice (see p. 101). Vary the amount of ancho chilies to taste.

Serves 8 (about ⅔ cup each)

4–6 ancho chilies, stems, seeds, and veins discarded
2 cups boiling water
4 medium tomatoes, cut into wedges
Vegetable cooking spray
2 pounds boneless beef eye of round steak, cut into ³⁄₄-inch cubes
1 large onion, chopped
2 cloves garlic, minced
1 teaspoon minced serrano, or jalapeño, chili
1 teaspoon dried oregano leaves
1 teaspoon cumin seed, crushed
2 tablespoons flour
Salt and pepper, to taste

1. Place ancho chilies in bowl; pour boiling water over. Let stand until chilies are softened, about 10 minutes. Process chilies, with water, and tomatoes in food processor or blender until smooth.

2. Spray large saucepan with cooking spray; heat over medium heat until hot. Cook beef until browned on all sides, about 5 minutes. Add onion, garlic, serrano chili, and herbs and cook until onion is tender, about 5 minutes. Stir in flour; cook over medium heat 1 to 2 minutes more.

3. Add chili and tomato mixture to saucepan; heat to boiling. Reduce heat and simmer, covered, until beef is tender, about 45 minutes. Season to taste with salt and pepper. Serve in shallow bowls.

Nutritional Data

PER SERVING		EXCHANGES	
Calories:	159	Milk:	0.0
% Calories from fat:	23	Vegetable:	1.0
Fat (gm):	4	Fruit:	0.0
Sat. fat (gm):	1.3	Bread:	0.0
Cholesterol (mg):	54.7	Meat:	2.5
Sodium (gm):	56	Fat:	0.0
Protein (gm):	22.1		
Carbohydrate (gm):	8.3		

BEEF STEAKS WITH TOMATILLO AND AVOCADO SAUCE

This sauce has much less avocado than the higher-fat Mexican version. We've added a bit of sour cream for richness and subtle flavor. The sauce would also be excellent with grilled or roasted poultry or lean pork.

Serves 6

Vegetable cooking spray
1 medium onion, thinly sliced
6 boneless beef eye of round steaks (about 4 ounces each)
1 cup Tomatillo Sauce (see p. 118)
2 tablespoons mashed avocado
2 tablespoons fat-free sour cream
6 flour, or corn, tortillas, warm

1. Spray large skillet with cooking spray; heat over medium heat until hot. Saute onion 2 to 3 minutes; reduce heat to medium-low and cook until onion is very soft, 5 to 8 minutes. Remove from skillet.

2. Add steaks to skillet; cook over medium heat to desired degree of doneness, 5 to 8 minutes on each side for medium.

3. Heat Tomatillo Sauce and avocado in small saucepan until hot; stir in sour cream.

4. Arrange steaks on serving platter; top with onions and spoon sauce over. Serve with tortillas.

Nutritional Data

PER SERVING		EXCHANGES	
Calories:	271	Milk:	0.0
% Calories from fat:	30	Vegetable:	1.0
Fat (gm):	8.9	Fruit:	0.0
Sat. fat (gm):	3.1	Bread:	1.0
Cholesterol (mg):	56.3	Meat:	3.0
Sodium (gm):	101	Fat:	0.0
Protein (gm):	28.2		
Carbohydrate (gm):	19.2		

MEXICAN HASH

A wonderful recipe for leftover meats or poultry! Add other vegetables, too, such as sliced zucchini and whole-kernel corn.

Serves 4

1 pound boneless beef eye of round steak, cut
   into ½-inch cubes
1 quart water
   Vegetable cooking spray
1 large tomato, chopped
2 large poblano chilies, sliced
1 large onion, chopped
1 pound Idaho potatoes, unpeeled, cooked, cut
   into ½-inch cubes
   Chili powder, to taste
   Salt and pepper, to taste

1. Heat beef cubes and water to boiling in large saucepan; reduce heat and simmer, covered, until beef is tender, 30 to 45 minutes. Drain; shred beef.

2. Spray large skillet with cooking spray; heat over medium heat until hot. Cook beef over medium-high heat until beginning to brown and crisp, about 5 minutes. Add tomato; cook over medium heat 5 more minutes. Remove from skillet and reserve.

3. Add poblano chilies and onion to skillet; cook until tender, 5 to 8 minutes. Add potatoes and cook until browned, about 5 minutes more. Add reserved meat mixture to skillet; cook until hot, 3 to 4 minutes. Season to taste with chili powder, salt, and pepper.

Nutritional Data

PER SERVING		EXCHANGES	
Calories:	242	Milk:	0.0
% Calories from fat:	15	Vegetable:	1.5
Fat (gm):	4	Fruit:	0.0
Sat. fat (gm):	1.3	Bread:	1.0
Cholesterol (mg):	54.7	Meat:	2.5
Sodium (gm):	55	Fat:	0.0
Protein (gm):	23.4		
Carbohydrate (gm):	27.90		

CHILI CON CARNE

◆

True Mexican chili con carne seldom has tomatoes; we've included tomatoes for American tastes, though you might try the chili without! Lean pork can be substituted for the beef; pinto or black beans can be substituted for the kidney beans.

Serves 6 (about 1 1/2 cups each)

1 1/2 pounds boneless beef eye of round, cut into
   1/2-inch cubes
1 1/2 quarts water
   Vegetable cooking spray
   6 ancho chilies, stems, seeds, and veins
   discarded
   1 large onion, chopped
   4 cloves garlic, minced
   4 medium tomatoes, chopped
   2 teaspoons dried oregano leaves
   3 cups cooked red kidney beans, or 2 cans (15
   ounces each) rinsed, drained red kidney beans
   Salt and pepper, to taste

1. Heat beef cubes and water to boiling in large saucepan; reduce heat and simmer, covered, until beef is tender, 30 to 45 minutes. Reserve in saucepan.

2. Spray a medium skillet with cooking spray; heat over medium heat until hot. Cook chilies over medium heat until softened; remove from skillet. Saute onion and garlic until tender, about 5 minutes. Add tomatoes and oregano and cook over medium heat until soft, 8 to 10 minutes.

3. Process chilies and vegetable mixture together in blender or food processor to a coarse puree. Add puree to beef mixture; heat to boiling. Reduce heat and simmer, uncovered, 20 minutes. Add beans and simmer, uncovered, 10 minutes or until desired consistency. Season to taste with salt and pepper.

Nutritional Data

PER SERVING		EXCHANGES	
Calories:	281	Milk:	0.0
% Calories from fat:	14	Vegetable:	2.0
Fat (gm):	4.6	Fruit:	0.0
Sat. fat (gm):	1.4	Bread:	1.0
Cholesterol (mg):	54.7	Meat:	3.0
Sodium (gm):	58	Fat:	0.0
Protein (gm):	30.3		
Carbohydrate (gm):	30.8		

6
SEAFOOD

Halibut with Sour Cream and Poblano Sauce

Crab Cakes with Poblano Chili Sauce

Grilled Fish with Chili Paste

Red Snapper Baked with Cilantro

Red Snapper Veracruz

Grilled Red Snapper with Tropical Salsa

Shrimp with Garlic Sauce

HALIBUT WITH SOUR CREAM AND POBLANO SAUCE

The versatile Sour Cream and Poblano Sauce also would be excellent served with shredded chicken breast or lean pork in soft tacos, or served over favorite enchiladas.

Serves 4

  1 pound halibut steaks
  3 tablespoons lime juice
  1 clove garlic, minced
1–2 tablespoons flour
     Vegetable cooking spray
     Salt and pepper, to taste
     Sour Cream and Poblano Sauce (recipe follows)
     Finely chopped cilantro, as garnish
  4 lime wedges

1. Place fish in glass baking dish. Combine lime juice and garlic; brush over fish. Refrigerate, covered, 1 hour.

2. Pat fish dry; coat lightly with flour. Generously spray large skillet with cooking spray; heat over medium heat until hot. Cook over medium heat until fish is lightly browned and flakes with a fork, 4 to 5 minutes on each side. Season lightly with salt and pepper.

3. Arrange fish on serving platter; spoon Sour Cream and Poblano Sauce over. Sprinkle with cilantro; serve with lime wedges.

Sour Cream and Poblano Sauce

     Vegetable cooking spray
  1 large poblano chili, veins and seeds discarded, thinly sliced
  1 small onion, finely chopped
  2 cloves garlic, minced
  1 cup fat-free sour cream
  ¼ teaspoon ground cumin
     Salt and pepper, to taste

1. Spray small saucepan with cooking spray; heat over medium heat until hot. Saute poblano chili, onion, and garlic until very tender, about 5 minutes. Stir in sour cream and cumin; cook over low heat until hot

through, 2 to 3 minutes. Season to taste with salt and pepper. Makes about 1 cup.

Nutritional Data

PER SERVING		EXCHANGES	
Calories:	184	Milk:	0.0
% Calories from fat:	13	Vegetable:	1.0
Fat (gm):	2.7	Fruit:	0.0
Sat. fat (gm):	0.4	Bread:	0.0
Cholesterol (mg):	36.4	Meat:	3.0
Sodium (gm):	101	Fat:	0.0
Protein (gm):	28.2		
Carbohydrate (gm):	11.9		

CRAB CAKES WITH POBLANO CHILI SAUCE

Shrimp or imitation crabmeat (surimi) can easily be substituted for all or part of the crab.

Serves 4

12 ounces Alaskan king crab, or peeled deveined shrimp, finely chopped
½ small onion, finely chopped
½ medium tomato, finely chopped
½ small jalapeño chili, seeds and veins discarded, minced
1 egg white
2–4 tablespoons dry unseasoned breadcrumbs
½ teaspoon dried oregano leaves
½ teaspoon salt (optional)
Flour, or dry unseasoned breadcrumbs
Vegetable Cooking Spray
½ cup Poblano Chili Sauce, or Enchilada Sauce (see pages 115 and 116)

1. Combine crab, onion, tomato, jalapeño chili, and egg white in small bowl; mix in breadcrumbs, oregano, and (optional) salt. Form mixture into 4 patties, each about ½ inch thick; coat lightly with flour or breadcrumbs.

2. Spray large skillet with cooking spray; heat over medium heat until hot. Cook patties over medium heat until cooked through and lightly browned, 3 to 4 minutes on each side.

3. Arrange crab cakes on serving dish; spoon Poblano Chili Sauce over.

Nutritional Data

PER SERVING		EXCHANGES	
Calories:	133	Milk:	0.0
% Calories from fat:	10	Vegetable:	2.0
Fat (gm):	1.4	Fruit:	0.0
Sat. fat (gm):	0.2	Bread:	0.0
Cholesterol (mg):	35.7	Meat:	2.0
Sodium (gm):	793	Fat:	0.0
Protein (gm):	18.6		
Carbohydrate (gm):	12.1		

GRILLED FISH WITH CHILI PASTE

♦

Dried ancho and pasilla chilies and vinegar combine to create a piquant seasoning for the fish.

Serves 4

1 pound fish fillets (any firm-fleshed white fish, red snapper, or tuna)
Chili Paste (recipe follows)
1 green onion and top, sliced
4 lime wedges

1. Spread top of fish with Chili Paste. Grill over hot coals, or broil 6 inches from heat source, until fish is tender and flakes with a fork, 10 to 15 minutes, depending upon thickness of fish.

2. Arrange fish on serving platter; sprinkle with green onion. Serve with lime wedges.

Chili Paste

Vegetable cooking spray
1 ancho chili
1 pasilla chili
2 cloves garlic, minced
½ teaspoon salt
1 tablespoon white wine vinegar
Water

1. Spray medium skillet with cooking spray; heat over medium heat until hot. Cook chilies over medium heat until softened, 1 to 2 minutes. Remove and discard stems, seeds, and veins.

2. Process chilies, garlic, salt, and vinegar in food processor or blender, adding a very small amount of water, if necessary, to make a smooth paste. Makes about ¼ cup.

Nutritional Data

PER SERVING		EXCHANGES	
Calories:	133	Milk:	0.0
% Calories from fat:	11	Vegetable:	0.5
Fat (gm):	1.5	Fruit:	0.0
Sat. fat (gm):	0.3	Bread:	0.0
Cholesterol (mg):	41.6	Meat:	2.5
Sodium (gm):	377	Fat:	0.0
Protein (gm):	23.4		
Carbohydrate (gm):	4.6		

RED SNAPPER BAKED WITH CILANTRO

Tuna, salmon, cod, or any firm-fleshed white fish can be used in this recipe.

Serves 6

1½ pounds red snapper fillets or steaks
⅓ cup lime juice
1½ tablespoons pickled jalapeño chili juice
1 teaspoon ground cumin
1 medium onion, thinly sliced
2 pickled jalapeño chilies, minced

   2 cloves garlic, minced
   1 cup coarsely chopped cilantro
      Salt and pepper, to taste
   6 lime wedges
      Green onion and top, thinly sliced, as garnish

1. Arrange fish in glass baking dish. Combine lime juice, jalapeño juice, and cumin; pour over fish. Arrange onion, jalapeño chilies, garlic, and cilantro over fish. Refrigerate, covered, 2 hours, turning fish once.

2. Bake, uncovered, at 400 degrees until fish is tender and flakes with a fork, about 10 minutes. Sprinkle fish lightly with salt and pepper. Arrange fish on serving platter with lime wedges. Sprinkle with green onion for garnish.

Nutritional Data

PER SERVING		EXCHANGES	
Calories:	135	Milk:	0.0
% Calories from fat:	12	Vegetable:	0.0
Fat (gm):	1.7	Fruit:	0.0
Sat. fat (gm):	0.3	Bread:	0.0
Cholesterol (mg):	41.6	Meat:	3.0
Sodium (gm):	169	Fat:	0.0
Protein (gm):	24		
Carbohydrate (gm):	5		

RED SNAPPER VERACRUZ

In this famous dish from Veracruz, red snapper is baked in a full-flavored tomato sauce with olives and capers. The fish can also be grilled, then topped with the sauce.

Serves 6

   1 whole red snapper, dressed (about 2 pounds)
   2 tablespoons lime juice
   2 cloves garlic, minced
      Veracruz Sauce (recipe follows)
   6 lime wedges, as garnish

1. Pierce surfaces of fish with long-tined fork; rub with lime juice and garlic. Refrigerate in large glass baking dish 2 hours.

2. Spoon Veracruz Sauce over fish. Bake, uncovered, at 400 degrees until fish is tender and flakes with a fork, 25 to 35 minutes. Place fish on serving plate; garnish with lime wedges.

Veracruz Sauce

        Vegetable cooking spray
    1   cup chopped onion
    3   cloves garlic, minced
    1   pickled jalapeño chili, minced
    2   cinnamon sticks, 1-inch pieces
    1   bay leaf
    ½   teaspoon dried oregano leaves
    ¼   teaspoon dried thyme leaves
    ¼   teaspoon ground cumin
    3   cups chopped tomatoes
    ¼   cup sliced, pitted green olives
  1–2   tablespoons rinsed, drained capers
        Salt and pepper, to taste

1. Spray large skillet with cooking spray; heat over medium heat until hot. Saute onion, garlic, jalapeño chili, cinnamon, and herbs until onion is tender, 5 to 8 minutes.

2. Add tomatoes, olives, and capers; cook, covered, over medium-high heat until tomatoes release liquid. Reduce heat and simmer, uncovered, until sauce is a medium consistency, about 10 minutes. Discard bay leaf; season to taste with salt and pepper. Makes about 2 cups.

Nutritional Data

PER SERVING		EXCHANGES	
Calories:	198	Milk:	0.0
% Calories from fat:	15	Vegetable:	2.0
Fat (gm):	3.3	Fruit:	0.0
Sat. fat (gm):	0.6	Bread:	0.0
Cholesterol (mg):	55.5	Meat:	3.0
Sodium (gm):	311	Fat:	0.0
Protein (gm):	32.6		
Carbohydrate (gm):	9.2		

GRILLED RED SNAPPER WITH TROPICAL SALSA

Though not traditional, the new trendy salsas are appearing in many resort restaurants in Mexico.

Serves 6

1 whole red snapper, dressed (about 2 pounds)
3 tablespoons lime juice
2 cloves garlic, minced
Tropical Salsa (recipe follows)
Lime wedges, as garnish
Cilantro, or parsley, sprigs, as garnish

1. Pierce surfaces of fish with long-tined fork; rub with lime juice and garlic. Refrigerate in large glass baking dish 2 hours.

2. Grill fish over medium-hot coals, or bake, uncovered, at 400 degrees until fish is tender and flakes with a fork, 20 to 25 minutes.

3. Arrange fish on serving platter; spoon Tropical Salsa around fish. Garnish with lime wedges and cilantro.

Tropical Salsa

$\frac{1}{2}$ cup cubed papaya, or mango
$\frac{1}{2}$ cup cubed pineapple
$\frac{1}{2}$ cup chopped tomato
$\frac{1}{4}$ cup chopped, seeded cucumber
$\frac{1}{4}$ cup cooked black beans
$\frac{1}{2}$ teaspoon minced jalapeño chili
2 tablespoons finely chopped cilantro
$\frac{1}{4}$ cup orange juice
1 tablespoon lime juice
2–3 teaspoons sugar

1. Combine papaya, pineapple, tomato, cucumber, black beans, jalapeño chili, and cilantro in small bowl. Combine orange and lime juice and sugar in separate bowl; add to other ingredients and toss. Refrigerate until serving time. Makes about 1$\frac{1}{2}$ cups.

Nutritional Data

PER SERVING		EXCHANGES	
Calories:	189	Milk:	0.0
% Calories from fat:	11	Vegetable:	0.0
Fat (gm):	2.2	Fruit:	0.5
Sat. fat (gm):	0.5	Bread:	0.0
Cholesterol (mg):	55.5	Meat:	3.0
Sodium (gm):	75	Fat:	0.0
Protein (gm):	32.1		
Carbohydrate (gm):	9		

SHRIMP WITH GARLIC SAUCE

The secret to the garlic sauce is to cook the garlic very slowly. The sauce is also excellent served over grilled or baked fish fillets or fish steaks.

Serves 4

1 pound peeled, deveined shrimp
2–3 tablespoons lime juice
1 large head garlic
2 tablespoons olive, or vegetable, oil
Salt and pepper, to taste
2 tablespoons finely chopped cilantro
Yellow Salsa Rice (see p. 98)
4 corn, or flour, tortillas

1. Arrange shrimp in glass dish; sprinkle with lime juice and refrigerate, covered, 30 minutes.

2. Peel garlic cloves and cut into halves. Heat oil in medium skillet until hot; add garlic and cook over low heat until garlic is soft and golden, 15 to 20 minutes. Remove garlic from skillet with slotted spoon.

3. Add shrimp to skillet; cook over medium to medium-high heat until shrimp are tender and pink, about 5 minutes. Return garlic to skillet; cook and stir over low heat 1 to 2 minutes. Season to taste with salt and pepper; sprinkle with cilantro. Serve with Yellow Salsa Rice and tortillas.

Nutritional Data

PER SERVING		EXCHANGES	
Calories:	388	Milk:	0.0
% Calories from fat:	20	Vegetable:	0.0
Fat (gm):	8.5	Fruit:	0.0
Sat. fat (gm):	1.3	Bread:	3.5
Cholesterol (mg):	131.6	Meat:	2.5
Sodium (gm):	340	Fat:	0.0
Protein (gm):	21.7		
Carbohydrate (gm):	55.1		

7
EGG AND CHEESE DISHES

Bean and Cheese Chiles Rellenos

Huevos Rancheros

Mexican Scrambled Eggs with Shrimp

Eggs Scrambled with Crisp Tortilla Strips

Eggs Scrambled with Cactus

BEAN AND CHEESE CHILES RELLENOS

Authentic chiles rellenos are made with poblano chilies.
Green bell (sweet) peppers can be substituted and the rellenos
will be delicious, but the flavor of the pepper is not the same.
Chiles rellenos are normally coated with a beaten egg-white
mixture and deep-fried in oil; our skinny version
uses only 1 tablespoon of vegetable oil.

Serves 6

6	large poblano chilies
2–3	quarts water
	Vegetable cooking spray
½	small jalapeño chili, seeds and veins discarded, minced
4	cloves garlic, minced
1	teaspoon dried oregano leaves
2	packages (8 ounces each) fat-free cream cheese, room temperature
½	cup (2 ounces) Mexican white cheese (*queso blanco*), or farmer's cheese, crumbled
1½	cups cooked pinto beans, or 1 can (15 ounces) pinto beans, rinsed, drained
1	tablespoon vegetable oil

1. Cut stems from tops of poblano chilies; remove and discard seeds and veins. Heat water to boiling in large saucepan; add peppers. Reduce heat and simmer, uncovered, 2 to 3 minutes, until peppers are slightly softened. Drain well and cool.

2. Spray small skillet with cooking spray; heat over medium heat until hot. Saute jalalpeño chili, garlic, and oregano until chili is tender, 2 to 3 minutes.

3. Mix cream cheese, white cheese, beans, and jalapeño chili mixture. Stuff poblano chilies with mixture. Heat oil in medium skillet until hot; saute peppers over medium to medium-high heat until tender and browned on all sides, 6 to 8 minutes. Serve hot.

Nutritional Data

PER SERVING		EXCHANGES	
Calories:	204	Milk:	0.0
% Calories from fat:	25	Vegetable:	1.0
Fat (gm):	5.5	Fruit:	0.0
Sat. fat (gm):	0.4	Bread:	1.0
Cholesterol (mg):	22.3	Meat:	1.5
Sodium (gm):	520	Fat:	0.5
Protein (gm):	17.2		
Carbohydrate (gm):	19.4		

HUEVOS RANCHEROS (COUNTRY-STYLE EGGS)

Everyone loves huevos rancheros—perfect for a hearty breakfast, brunch, or light supper.

Serves 6

6 corn tortillas
   Vegetable cooking spray
6 eggs
   Salt and pepper, to taste
   Serrano Tomato Sauce (recipe follows)
   Refried Beans (see p. 102)

1. Spray tortillas lightly with cooking spray; cook in large skillet until browned, about 1 minute on each side.

2. Spray large skillet with cooking spray; heat over medium heat until hot. Add eggs, sunny side up. Reduce heat to medium-low and cook, covered, until eggs are glazed on top, 3 to 4 minutes. Season to taste with salt and pepper.

3. Arrange tortillas on serving plates; place eggs on tortillas and spoon Serrano Tomato Sauce over. Serve with Refried Beans.

Serrano Tomato Sauce

2 large tomatoes, cut into wedges
   Vegetable cooking spray
1 small onion, finely chopped
1 serrano chili, seeds and veins discarded, minced

1 clove garlic, minced
Salt, to taste

1. Process tomatoes in food processor or blender until almost smooth.

2. Spray medium skillet with cooking spray; heat over medium heat until hot. Saute onion, serrano chili, and garlic until tender, 3 to 4 minutes. Add tomato and heat to boiling; cook over medium to medium-high heat until mixture thickens to a medium sauce consistency. Season to taste with salt; serve warm. Makes about 2 cups.

Nutritional Data

PER SERVING		EXCHANGES	
Calories:	252	Milk:	0.0
% Calories from fat:	22	Vegetable:	1.0
Fat (gm):	6.2	Fruit:	0.0
Sat. fat (gm):	1.7	Bread:	2.0
Cholesterol (mg):	213	Meat:	1.5
Sodium (gm):	109	Fat:	0.0
Protein (gm):	14.3		
Carbohydrate (gm):	35.6		

MEXICAN SCRAMBLED EGGS WITH SHRIMP

*Substitute Chorizo (see p. 70) for the shrimp
in this recipe if you prefer.*

Serves 4

Vegetable cooking spray
1 medium tomato, chopped
¼ cup sliced green onions and tops
1–2 teaspoons finely chopped serrano, or jalapeño, chilies
1 small clove garlic, minced
8 ounces peeled, deveined shrimp
4 eggs
4 egg whites, or ½ cup cholesterol-free egg substitute
2 tablespoons skim milk
Salt and pepper, to taste

1 cup (½ recipe) Tomatillo Sauce, warm (see
p. 118)
4 corn, or flour, tortillas

1. Spray large skillet with cooking spray; heat over medium heat until
hot. Saute tomato, green onions, serrano chili, and garlic until tender,
about 5 minutes. Add shrimp and cook over medium heat until shrimp
are pink and cooked, 3 to 4 minutes.

2. Beat eggs, egg whites, and skim milk until foamy; add to skillet. Cook
over medium to medium-low heat until eggs are cooked, stirring
occasionally; season to taste with salt and pepper. Serve with Tomatillo
Sauce and tortillas.

Nutritional Data

PER SERVING		EXCHANGES	
Calories:	243	Milk:	0.0
% Calories from fat:	26	Vegetable:	1.0
Fat (gm):	7.1	Fruit:	0.0
Sat. fat (gm):	1.8	Bread:	1.0
Cholesterol (mg):	300.6	Meat:	2.5
Sodium (gm):	268	Fat:	0.0
Protein (gm):	22.3		
Carbohydrate (gm):	22.5		

EGGS SCRAMBLED WITH CRISP TORTILLA STRIPS

*This is a good recipe to use with day-old or slightly stale
tortillas. Complement this hearty egg dish with Refried Beans
and Chorizo (see pages 102 and 70).*

Serves 6

6 corn tortillas, cut into 2 x ½-inch strips
Vegetable cooking spray
6 eggs
6 egg whites, or ¾ cup cholesterol-free egg
substitute
3 tablespoons skim milk
Salt and pepper, to taste
3 tablespoons crumbled Mexican white cheese,
or farmer's cheese

3 tablespoons finely chopped cilantro
1½ cups Poblano Chili Sauce, warm (see p. 115)
Black Beans and Rice (see p. 101)

1. Spray tortilla strips lightly with cooking spray; cook in skillet over medium to medium-high heat until browned and crisp.

2. Beat eggs, egg whites, and milk until foamy; pour over tortilla strips in skillet. Cook over medium to medium-low heat until eggs are cooked, stirring occasionally. Season to taste with salt and pepper; sprinkle with cheese and cilantro. Spoon Poblano Chili Sauce over eggs; serve with Black Beans and Rice.

Nutritional Data

PER SERVING		EXCHANGES	
Calories:	367	Milk:	0.0
% Calories from fat:	18	Vegetable:	1.0
Fat (gm):	7.7	Fruit:	0.0
Sat. fat (gm):	2.2	Bread:	3.0
Cholesterol (mg):	215.7	Meat:	2.5
Sodium (gm):	480	Fat:	0.0
Protein (gm):	22.9		
Carbohydrate (gm):	55.9		

EGGS SCRAMBLED WITH CACTUS

Cactus paddles, or nopales, are available canned as well as fresh; the canned cactus do not have to be cooked. Poblano chilies or sweet bell peppers can be substituted, if preferred.

Serves 4

1 quart boiling water
8 ounces cactus paddles, sliced
1 teaspoon salt
¼ teaspoon baking soda
Vegetable cooking spray
1 small tomato, chopped
1 cup chopped onion
1 teaspoon finely chopped jalapeño chili
4 eggs

4 egg whites, or ½ cup cholesterol-free egg
   substitute
2 tablespoons skim milk
   Salt and pepper, to taste
4 corn, or flour, tortillas, warm

1. Heat water to boiling in medium saucepan; add cactus, 1 teaspoon salt, and baking soda. Reduce heat and simmer, uncovered, until cactus is crisp-tender, about 20 minutes. Rinse well in cold water and drain.

2. Spray large skillet with cooking spray; heat over medium heat until hot. Saute cactus, tomato, onion, and jalapeño chili until onion is tender, 3 to 4 minutes.

3. Beat eggs, egg whites, and skim milk until foamy; add to skillet. Cook over medium to medium-low heat until eggs are cooked, stirring occasionally. Season to taste with salt and pepper. Serve with tortillas.

Nutritional Data

PER SERVING		EXCHANGES	
Calories:	179	Milk:	0.0
% Calories from fat:	29	Vegetable:	1.0
Fat (gm):	5.8	Fruit:	0.0
Sat. fat (gm):	1.7	Bread:	1.0
Cholesterol (mg):	213.1	Meat:	2.0
Sodium (gm):	258	Fat:	0.0
Protein (gm):	12.7		
Carbohydrate (gm):	18.7		

8
RICE, BEANS, AND VEGETABLE SIDE DISHES

Yellow Salsa Rice

Orange Cilantro Rice

Mexican Red Rice

Black Beans and Rice

Refried Beans

Zucchini from Puebla

Potatoes with Poblano Chilies

Chayote with Pepitas

Stuffed Cabbage with Chili Tomato Sauce

Corn Pudding

Carrot Pudding

Jicama Salad

Cactus Salad

YELLOW SALSA RICE

*Ground turmeric contributes subtle flavor and
an attractive yellow color to the rice.*

Serves 6 (about ⅔ cup each)

1 can (14½ ounces) fat-free, reduced-sodium
   chicken broth
⅓ cup water
½ teaspoon ground turmeric
1 cup long-grain rice
¼ cup prepared medium, or hot, salsa
1 medium tomato, chopped
   Salt and pepper, to taste
   Cilantro, or parsley, finely chopped, as garnish

1. Heat chicken broth, water, and turmeric to boiling in medium
   saucepan; stir in rice and salsa. Reduce heat and simmer, covered,
   until rice is tender and liquid absorbed, 20 to 25 minutes; stir in
   tomato during last 5 minutes of cooking time. Season to taste with salt
   and pepper.

2. Spoon rice into serving bowl; sprinkle with cilantro.

Nutritional Data

PER SERVING		EXCHANGES	
Calories:	126	Milk:	0.0
% Calories from fat:	2	Vegetable:	1.0
Fat (gm):	0.3	Fruit:	0.0
Sat. fat (gm):	0.1	Bread:	1.5
Cholesterol (mg):	0.3	Meat:	0.0
Sodium (gm):	99	Fat:	0.0
Protein (gm):	3.8		
Carbohydrate (gm):	26.6		

ORANGE CILANTRO RICE

◆

*A perfect accompaniment to grilled or
roasted lean meats or poultry.*

Serves 6 (about ⅔ cup each)

Vegetable cooking spray
½ cup sliced green onions and tops
1 cup long-grain rice
Zest of 1 small orange, grated
2¼ cups water
2 tablespoons finely chopped cilantro
Salt and pepper, to taste

1. Spray medium saucepan with cooking spray; heat over medium heat until hot. Saute onions until tender, 3 to 5 minutes. Add rice and orange zest to saucepan; cook over medium heat until rice is lightly browned, 2 to 3 minutes, stirring frequently.

2. Add water to saucepan and heat to boiling; reduce heat and simmer, covered, until rice is tender, 20 to 25 minutes. Stir in cilantro; season to taste with salt and pepper.

Nutritional Data

PER SERVING		EXCHANGES	
Calories:	118	Milk:	0.0
% Calories from fat:	1	Vegetable:	0.0
Fat (gm):	0.2	Fruit:	0.0
Sat. fat (gm):	0	Bread:	1.5
Cholesterol (mg):	0	Meat:	0.0
Sodium (gm):	2	Fat:	0.0
Protein (gm):	2.3		
Carbohydrate (gm):	26		

MEXICAN RED RICE

◆

The tomatoes are pureed in the traditional version of this recipe.
We've chosen to chop the tomatoes for color and flavor.

Serves 6 (about ⅔ cup each)

Vegetable cooking spray
1 large tomato, chopped
½ cup chopped onion
1 clove garlic, minced
½ teaspoon dried oregano leaves
¼ teaspoon ground cumin
1 cup long-grain rice
1 can (14½ ounces) fat-free, reduced-sodium
  chicken broth
⅓ cup water
1 carrot, cooked, diced
½ cup frozen, thawed peas
Salt and pepper, to taste

1. Coat large saucepan with cooking spray; heat over medium heat until
hot. Saute tomato, onion, garlic, and herbs until onion is tender, 3 to 5
minutes. Add rice; cook over medium heat until rice is lightly
browned, 2 to 3 minutes, stirring frequently.

2. Add broth and water to saucepan; heat to boiling. Reduce heat and
simmer, covered, until rice is tender, about 25 minutes, adding carrot
and peas during last 5 minutes. Season to taste with salt and pepper.

Nutritional Data

PER SERVING		EXCHANGES	
Calories:	146	Milk:	0.0
% Calories from fat:	2	Vegetable:	0.0
Fat (gm):	0.4	Fruit:	0.0
Sat. fat (gm):	0.1	Bread:	2.0
Cholesterol (mg):	0	Meat:	0.0
Sodium (gm):	41	Fat:	0.0
Protein (gm):	4.7		
Carbohydrate (gm):	30.7		

BLACK BEANS AND RICE

◆

Serve this hearty rice with grilled lean meats or poultry, or with stews, such as Beef and Ancho Chili Stew (see p. 73). If fresh epazote is available, add a sprig or two to the rice while cooking.

Serves 6 (about ⅔ cup each)

Vegetable cooking spray
¼ cup chopped onion
¼ cup sliced green onions and tops
4 cloves garlic, minced
1 cup long-grain rice
2½ cups fat-free, reduced-sodium chicken broth
1 can (15 ounces) black beans, rinsed, drained
2 tablespoons finely chopped cilantro
Salt and pepper, to taste

1. Spray medium saucepan with cooking spray; heat over medium heat until hot. Saute onion, green onions, and garlic until tender, about 5 minutes. Add rice; cook over medium heat until rice is lightly browned, 2 to 3 minutes, stirring frequently.

2. Add chicken broth to saucepan and heat to boiling; reduce heat and simmer, covered, until rice is tender, 20 to 25 minutes, adding beans during last 5 minutes. Stir in cilantro; season to taste with salt and pepper.

Nutritional Data

PER SERVING		EXCHANGES	
Calories:	186	Milk:	0.0
% Calories from fat:	4	Vegetable:	0.0
Fat (gm):	0.8	Fruit:	0.0
Sat. fat (gm):	0.1	Bread:	2.5
Cholesterol (mg):	0	Meat:	0.0
Sodium (gm):	253	Fat:	0.0
Protein (gm):	10.1		
Carbohydrate (gm):	38.8		

REFRIED BEANS

Two cans (15 ounces each) of pinto beans, rinsed and drained, can be substituted for the dried beans. Then make the recipe, beginning with Step 2, substituting 1 can (14 1/2 ounces) of fat-free, reduced-sodium chicken broth for the cooking liquid.

Serves 6 (about 1/2 cup each)

1 1/4 cups dried pinto beans
Water
Vegetable cooking spray
1 medium onion, coarsely chopped
Salt and pepper, to taste

1. Wash and sort beans, discarding any stones. Cover beans with 2 inches of water in a large saucepan; heat to boiling and boil, uncovered, 2 minutes. Remove from heat; let stand, covered, 1 hour. Drain beans; cover with 2 inches of water and heat to boiling. Reduce heat and simmer, covered, until beans are tender, 1 1/2 to 2 hours. Drain, reserving 2 cups liquid.

2. Spray large skillet with cooking spray; heat over medium heat until hot. Saute onion until tender, 3 to 5 minutes. Add 1 cup beans and 1 cup reserved liquid to skillet. Cook over high heat, mashing beans until almost smooth with end of meat mallet or potato masher. Add half the remaining beans and liquid; continue cooking and mashing beans. Repeat with remaining beans and liquid. Season to taste with salt and pepper.

Nutritional Data

PER SERVING		EXCHANGES	
Calories:	106	Milk:	0.0
% Calories from fat:	3	Vegetable:	0.0
Fat (gm):	0.4	Fruit:	0.0
Sat. fat (gm):	0.1	Bread:	1.5
Cholesterol (mg):	0	Meat:	0.0
Sodium (gm):	2	Fat:	0.0
Protein (gm):	6.1		
Carbohydrate (gm):	20		

ZUCCHINI FROM PUEBLA

If the Mexican white cheese, queso blanco, is not available, farmer's cheese can be readily substituted. Purchased roasted peppers can be used.

Serves 6 (about 1/2 cup each)

Vegetable cooking spray
1 cup chopped onion
2 pounds zucchini, cut diagonally into 1/4-inch slices
4 roasted red bell peppers, cut into strips (about 1 cup)
1/2 cup fat-free, reduced-sodium chicken broth
1/2–1 teaspoon ground cumin
1/2 cup skim milk
Salt and pepper, to taste
2 tablespoons crumbled Mexican white cheese, or farmer's cheese

1. Spray large skillet with cooking spray; heat over medium heat until hot. Saute onion until tender, 5 to 8 minutes. Stir in zucchini, roasted peppers, broth, and cumin. Heat to boiling. Reduce heat and simmer, covered, just until zucchini is crisp-tender, 5 to 8 minutes.

2. Add milk; cook until hot, 1 to 2 minutes. Season to taste with salt and pepper. Spoon zucchini and broth into serving bowl; sprinkle with cheese.

Nutritional Data

PER SERVING		EXCHANGES	
Calories:	100	Milk:	0.0
% Calories from fat:	11	Vegetable:	4.0
Fat (gm):	1.4	Fruit:	0.0
Sat. fat (gm):	0	Bread:	0.0
Cholesterol (mg):	2.6	Meat:	0.0
Sodium (gm):	36	Fat:	0.0
Protein (gm):	5.1		
Carbohydrate (gm):	20.3		

POTATOES WITH POBLANO CHILIES

◆

In this recipe, roasted poblano chilies are combined with potatoes for a hearty side dish. Serve with any meat dish, or with a fried egg and salsa for brunch.

Serves 4 (about ²/₃ cup each)

4 medium poblano chilies
  Vegetable cooking spray
1 medium onion, sliced
1 pound Idaho potatoes, unpeeled, cooked, cut
  into ¹/₂-inch cubes
  Salt and pepper, to taste

1. Cut chilies into halves; discard stems, seeds, and veins. Place chilies, skin sides up, on broiler pan; broil 6 inches from heat source until skin is blackened and blistered. Wrap chilies in plastic bag or paper toweling 5 minutes; peel off skin and discard. Cut chilies into strips.

2. Coat large skillet with cooking spray; heat over medium heat until hot. Saute onion 2 to 3 minutes; add chilies and potatoes. Cook over medium heat until onion is tender and potatoes browned, 5 to 8 minutes. Season to taste with salt and pepper.

Nutritional Data

PER SERVING		EXCHANGES	
Calories:	147	Milk:	0.0
% Calories from fat:	2	Vegetable:	1.0
Fat (gm):	0.3	Fruit:	0.0
Sat. fat (gm):	0.1	Bread:	1.5
Cholesterol (mg):	0	Meat:	0.0
Sodium (gm):	11	Fat:	0.0
Protein (gm):	3.7		
Carbohydrate (gm):	34		

CHAYOTE WITH PEPITAS

The pumpkin seeds (pepitas) will begin to pop and jump in the skillet, signaling that they are toasted! Chayote squash have the crisp texture of an apple when raw and can be sauteed or steamed until crisp-tender.

Serves 4

Vegetable cooking spray

4 teaspoons pumpkin seeds

½ cup finely chopped onion

2 cloves garlic, minced

2 chayote squash, peeled, pitted, cut into ½-inch cubes

Salt and pepper, to taste

1. Spray small skillet with vegetable cooking spray; heat over medium heat until hot. Cook pumpkin seeds over medium heat until they are toasted and begin to pop, 3 to 5 minutes. Reserve.

2. Spray large skillet with vegetable cooking spray; heat over medium heat until hot. Saute onion and garlic until tender, 3 to 5 minutes. Add squash and cook over medium heat until squash is crisp-tender, about 20 minutes, stirring occasionally. Season to taste with salt and pepper. Spoon squash into serving bowl; sprinkle with reserved pumpkin seeds.

Nutritional Data

PER SERVING		EXCHANGES	
Calories:	35	Milk:	0.0
% Calories from fat:	16	Vegetable:	1.5
Fat (gm):	0.7	Fruit:	0.0
Sat. fat (gm):	0.1	Bread:	0.0
Cholesterol (mg):	0	Meat:	0.0
Sodium (gm):	2	Fat:	0.0
Protein (gm):	1.1		
Carbohydrate (gm):	7		

STUFFED CABBAGE WITH CHILI TOMATO SAUCE

This dish can also be served in larger portions as a vegetarian entree. Or a cooked, shredded meat such as pork or beef can be added to the rice.

Serves 12 (as side dish)

1 large green cabbage
1 large onion, chopped
1 clove garlic, minced
1/4–1/2 jalapeño chili, seeds and veins discarded, minced
1 tablespoon vegetable oil
3/4 teaspoon dried oregano leaves
1/2 teaspoon dried thyme leaves
1 can (15 ounces) black beans, rinsed, drained
2 medium tomatoes, chopped
1/2 cup cooked rice
1/2 cup raisins
1 tablespoon finely chopped cilantro
Salt and pepper, to taste
Chili Tomato Sauce (see p. 114)

1. Trim cabbage, discarding any wilted outside leaves. Place cabbage in large saucepan with water to cover; heat to boiling. Reduce heat and simmer, covered, 10 minutes. Drain cabbage; cool until warm enough to handle.

2. In a large skillet, saute onion, garlic, and jalapeño chili in oil until tender, about 5 minutes. Add oregano and thyme; cook 1 minute longer.

3. Add beans and tomatoes to skillet; cook over medium heat, lightly mashing beans with a fork, until tomatoes release liquid, about 10 minutes. Stir in rice, raisins, and cilantro; season to taste with salt and pepper.

4. Place cabbage on large square of double-thickness cheesecloth. Spread outer cabbage leaves as flat as possible without breaking them off. Cut out inner leaves of cabbage, chop them finely, and add to rice mixture; remove and discard core of cabbage.

5. Pack rice mixture into center of the cabbage; fold outer leaves up over mixture, reshaping cabbage. Gather up cheesecloth around cabbage and tie with string. Place cabbage in large saucepan and add water to cover; heat to boiling. Reduce heat and simmer, covered, 1 hour. Lift cabbage from saucepan and remove cheesecloth.

6. Place cabbage on serving plate; cut into wedges. Serve with Chili Tomato Sauce.

Nutritional Data

PER SERVING		EXCHANGES	
Calories:	111	Milk:	0.0
% Calories from fat:	14	Vegetable:	3.0
Fat (gm):	2	Fruit:	0.0
Sat. fat (gm):	0.2	Bread:	0.5
Cholesterol (mg):	0	Meat:	0.0
Sodium (gm):	157	Fat:	0.0
Protein (gm):	5.7		
Carbohydrate (gm):	22.2		

CORN PUDDING

Serve hot with a grilled meat or poultry. Also try it with Chili Tomato Sauce (see p. 114) or dollops of fat-free sour cream.

Serves 6 (about ½ cup each)

Vegetable cooking spray
2 tablespoons plain dry breadcrumbs
2 cups fresh, or frozen and thawed, whole kernel corn
½ cup skim milk
3 tablespoons flour
1 ½ tablespoons margarine, softened
1 egg
2 egg whites
1 teaspoon sugar
¼ teaspoon dried thyme leaves
¼ teaspoon ground cumin
½ teaspoon salt
⅛ teaspoon pepper

1. Spray 1-quart casserole or souffle dish with cooking spray; coat dish with breadcrumbs.

2. Process corn, milk, and flour in food processor or blender until a coarse puree. Beat margarine, egg, and egg whites until smooth in medium bowl; mix in sugar, herbs, salt, and pepper. Stir in corn mixture and pour all into prepared casserole.

3. Bake, uncovered, at 350 degrees until pudding is set and beginning to brown, about 35 minutes. Serve immediately.

Nutritional Data

PER SERVING		EXCHANGES	
Calories:	122	Milk:	0.0
% Calories from fat:	28	Vegetable:	0.0
Fat (gm):	3.9	Fruit:	0.0
Sat. fat (gm):	0.9	Bread:	1.0
Cholesterol (mg):	35.8	Meat:	0.5
Sodium (gm):	272	Fat:	0.5
Protein (gm):	5.3		
Carbohydrate (gm):	17.9		

CARROT PUDDING

This recipe is being included as a side dish although it is served as a dessert in Mexico.

Serves 8

    2 pounds carrots, cooked, mashed
    ½ cup sugar
    1½ tablespoons margarine, melted
    ½ cup all-purpose flour
    1½ teaspoons baking powder
    ½ teaspoon ground cinnamon
    ½ teaspoon salt
    ½ cup raisins
    ½ cup (2 ounces) shredded fat-free Cheddar
        cheese
    4 egg whites, beaten to stiff peaks
    ¼ cup sliced almonds (optional)

1. Mix carrots, sugar, and margarine in medium bowl. Combine flour, baking powder, cinnamon, and salt and add to carrot mixture. Mix in raisins and cheese; fold in beaten egg whites. Spoon mixture into 8-inch-square baking pan; sprinkle with almonds.

2. Bake at 475 degrees 10 minutes; reduce temperature to 350 degrees and bake until browned and set, 50 to 60 minutes. Cut into squares.

Nutritional Data

PER SERVING		EXCHANGES	
Calories:	191	Milk:	0.0
% Calories from fat:	11	Vegetable:	1.5
Fat (gm):	2.5	Fruit:	0.5
Sat. fat (gm):	0.5	Bread:	1.5
Cholesterol (mg):	1.3	Meat:	0.0
Sodium (gm):	339	Fat:	0.5
Protein (gm):	6.3		
Carbohydrate (gm):	37.9		

JICAMA SALAD

Jicama adds a marvelous crispness to salads, complementing both fruits and vegetables.

Serves 6 (about ⅔ cup each)

½ large jicama, peeled (about 12 ounces)
½ medium zucchini, sliced
1 small orange, cut into segments
2–3 thin slices red onion
    Cilantro Lime Dressing (recipe follows)
    Salt and pepper, to taste
    Lettuce leaves, as garnish

1. Cut jicama into sticks about 1½ x ½ inches. Combine jicama, zucchini, orange, and onion in bowl. Pour Cilantro Lime Dressing over and toss; season to taste with salt and pepper.

2. Arrange lettuce leaves on salad plates; top with salad mixture.

Cilantro Lime Dressing

2 tablespoons lime juice
1 tablespoon orange juice
1–2 tablespoons olive, or vegetable, oil
2 tablespoons finely chopped cilantro
2 teaspoons sugar

1. Combine all ingredients. Refrigerate until serving time; mix before using. Makes about ¼ cup.

Nutritional Data

PER SERVING		EXCHANGES	
Calories:	77	Milk:	0.0
% Calories from fat:	27	Vegetable:	1.0
Fat (gm):	2.4	Fruit:	0.5
Sat. fat (gm):	0.3	Bread:	0.0
Cholesterol (mg):	0	Meat:	0.0
Sodium (gm):	1	Fat:	0.5
Protein (gm):	1.3		
Carbohydrate (gm):	13.5		

CACTUS SALAD

The tender cactus paddles, nopales, are readily available in large supermarkets today—be sure all the thorns have been removed! If not, they can be pulled out easily with tweezers.

Serves 6 (about ½ cup each)

2 quarts water
1½ pounds cactus paddles, cut into ½-inch pieces
1 tablespoon salt
¼ teaspoon baking soda
1½ cups cherry tomato halves
½ cup thinly sliced red onion
Lime Dressing (recipe follows)
Lettuce leaves, as garnish

1. Heat water to boiling in large saucepan; add cactus, salt, and baking soda. Reduce heat and simmer, uncovered, until cactus is crisp-tender, about 20 minutes. Rinse well in cold water and drain thoroughly.

2. Combine cactus, tomatoes, and onion in small bowl; pour Lime Dressing over and toss. Serve on lettuce-lined plates.

Lime Dressing

2 tablespoons lime juice
1–2 tablespoons olive, or vegetable, oil
1 tablespoon water
1 teaspoon cider vinegar
2 teaspoons sugar
½ teaspoon dried oregano leaves

l. Combine all ingredients; refrigerate until serving time. Makes about ¼ cup.

Nutritional Data

PER SERVING		EXCHANGES	
Calories:	78	Milk:	0.0
% Calories from fat:	28	Vegetable:	2.0
Fat (gm):	2.5	Fruit:	0.0
Sat. fat (gm):	0.3	Bread:	0.0
Cholesterol (mg):	0	Meat:	0.0
Sodium (gm):	131	Fat:	0.5
Protein (gm):	2.4		
Carbohydrate (gm):	12.5		

9
SAUCES

Chili Tomato Sauce

Poblano Chili Sauce

Enchilada Sauce

Jalapeño con Queso Sauce

Tomatillo Sauce

Mole Sauce

CHILI TOMATO SAUCE

———————◆———————

A very simple but versatile sauce that can be used with tacos,
enchiladas, and roasted or grilled meats and poultry.

Serves 8 (¼ cup each)

1 can (16 ounces) reduced-sodium tomato sauce
¼ cup water
2–2½ tablespoons chili powder
2 cloves garlic
Salt and pepper, to taste

1. Combine tomato sauce, water, chili powder, and garlic in small saucepan; heat to boiling. Reduce heat and simmer, uncovered, 2 to 3 minutes. Season to taste with salt and pepper. Makes 2 cups.

Nutritional Data

PER SERVING		EXCHANGES	
Calories:	30	Milk:	0.0
% Calories from fat:	10	Vegetable:	0.8
Fat (gm):	0.3	Fruit:	0.0
Sat. fat (gm):	0	Bread:	0.0
Cholesterol (mg):	0	Meat:	0.0
Sodium (gm):	36	Fat:	0.0
Protein (gm):	1.3		
Carbohydrate (gm):	5.9		

POBLANO CHILI SAUCE

---

*Fast and easy to make, this sauce will vary
in hotness depending upon the individual poblano
chili and the amount of chili powder used.*

Serves 8 (¼ cup each)

Vegetable cooking spray
2 medium tomatoes, chopped
½ medium poblano chili, seeds and veins
   discarded, chopped
1 small onion, chopped
2 cloves garlic, minced
1–2 tablespoons chili powder
Salt and pepper, to taste

1. Spray large skillet with cooking spray; heat over medium heat until hot. Cook tomatoes, poblano chili, onion, garlic, and chili powder until poblano chili and onion are very tender, 8 to 10 minutes.

2. Process mixture in food processor or blender until smooth; season to taste with salt and pepper. Makes about 2 cups.

Nutritional Data

PER SERVING		EXCHANGES	
Calories:	16	Milk:	0.0
% Calories from fat:	14	Vegetable:	0.5
Fat (gm):	0.3	Fruit:	0.0
Sat. fat (gm):	0	Bread:	0.0
Cholesterol (mg):	0	Meat:	0.0
Sodium (gm):	13	Fat:	0.0
Protein (gm):	0.6		
Carbohydrate (gm):	3.4		

ENCHILADA SAUCE

*Many Mexican sauces are a simple combination
of pureed ingredients that are then cooked or "fried"
until thickened to desired consistency.*

Serves 8 (¼ cup each)

1 ancho chili, stem, seeds, and veins discarded
  Boiling water
2 medium tomatoes, chopped
1 red bell pepper, chopped
1 small onion, chopped
2 cloves garlic, minced
½ teaspoon dried marjoram leaves
⅛ teaspoon ground allspice
  Vegetable cooking spray
1 bay leaf
  Salt, to taste

1. Cover ancho chili with boiling water in small bowl; let stand until softened, 10 to 15 minutes. Drain.

2. Process ancho chili, tomatoes, bell pepper, onion, garlic, marjoram, and allspice in food processor or blender until almost smooth.

3. Spray small skillet with cooking spray; heat over medium heat until hot. "Fry" sauce and bay leaf over medium heat until thickened to a medium consistency; discard bay leaf and season to taste with salt. Serve hot. Makes about 2 cups.

Nutritional Data

PER SERVING		EXCHANGES	
Calories:	15	Milk:	0.0
% Calories from fat:	8	Vegetable:	0.0
Fat (gm):	0.2	Fruit:	0.0
Sat. fat (gm):	0	Bread:	0.0
Cholesterol (mg):	0	Meat:	0.0
Sodium (gm):	3.6	Fat:	0.0
Protein (gm):	0.6		
Carbohydrate (gm):	3.4		

JALAPEÑO CON QUESO SAUCE

A versatile sauce to enhance enchiladas and other tortilla dishes. This goes especially well with Potatoes with Poblano Chilies (see p. 104).

Serves 8 (¼ cup each)

Vegetable cooking spray
1 teaspoon finely chopped jalapeño chili
1 teaspoon ground cumin
½ teaspoon dried oregano leaves
8 ounces reduced-fat pasteurized processed cheese product, cubed
⅓–½ cup skim milk
1¼ cups (5 ounces) shredded fat-free Cheddar cheese

1. Spray medium saucepan with cooking spray; heat over medium heat until hot. Saute jalapeño chili until tender, about 2 minutes; stir in cumin and oregano.

2. Add processed cheese product; cook over low heat, stirring frequently, until melted. Stir in ⅓ cup milk and Cheddar cheese. Stir in additional milk if needed for desired consistency, cooking until hot through, 1 to 2 minutes. Makes about 2 cups.

Nutritional Data

PER SERVING		EXCHANGES	
Calories:	92	Milk:	0.0
% Calories from fat:	30	Vegetable:	0.0
Fat (gm):	3.2	Fruit:	0.0
Sat. fat (gm):	2	Bread:	0.0
Cholesterol (mg):	13.4	Meat:	2.0
Sodium (gm):	562	Fat:	0.0
Protein (gm):	12.2		
Carbohydrate (gm):	4.4		

TOMATILLO SAUCE

◆

*Made with Mexican green tomatoes (tomatillos), this sauce
is very fast and easy to make. It can be served over chicken,
fish, pork, flautas, enchiladas, and tacos.*

Serves 8 (¼ cup each)

1½ pounds tomatillos
    Water
 ½ medium onion, chopped
  1 clove garlic, minced
 ½ small serrano chili, minced
  3 tablespoons finely chopped cilantro
    Vegetable cooking spray
2–3 teaspoons sugar
    Salt and white pepper, to taste

1. Remove and discard husks from *tomatillos*. Simmer, covered, in 1 inch of water in large saucepan until tender, 5 to 8 minutes. Cool; drain.

2. Process *tomatillos*, onion, garlic, serrano chili, and cilantro in food processor or blender, using pulse technique, until almost smooth. Spray large skillet with cooking spray; heat over medium heat until hot. Add sauce and "fry" over medium heat until slightly thickened, about 5 minutes. Season to taste with sugar, salt, and pepper. Makes 2 cups.

Nutritional Data

PER SERVING		EXCHANGES	
Calories:	38	Milk:	0.0
% Calories from fat:	19	Vegetable:	2.0
Fat (gm):	1.0	Fruit:	0.0
Sat. fat (gm):	0	Bread:	0.0
Cholesterol (mg):	0	Meat:	0.0
Sodium (gm):	2	Fat:	0.0
Protein (gm):	1.2		
Carbohydrate (gm):	7.6		

MOLE SAUCE

Mole is the most popular and traditional of all the Mexican sauces, usually served with turkey. Piquant with chilies and fragrant with sweet spices, the sauce is also flavored with unsweetened chocolate. Even this simplified version of the delicious mole is somewhat time consuming to make, so double the recipe and freeze half!

Serves 8 (¹/₃ cup each)

Vegetable cooking spray
3 mulato chilies
4 ancho chilies
4 pasilla chilies
   Boiling water
1 tablespoon sesame seed
4 whole peppercorns
2 whole cloves
¹/₈ teaspoon coriander seed
¹/₂ -inch piece cinnamon stick
2 tablespoons raisins
2 tablespoons whole, or slivered, almonds
2 tablespoons pumpkin seed
¹/₄ cup chopped onion
2 cloves garlic, finely chopped
1 small corn tortilla
1 small tomato, chopped
1–1¹/₂ cups fat-free, reduced-sodium chicken broth, divided
1–2 tablespoons unsweetened cocoa
   Salt, to taste

1. Spray medium skillet with cooking spray; heat over medium heat until hot. Cook all chilies over medium heat until softened; remove and discard stems, seeds, and veins (if chilies are already soft, the cooking step can be omitted). Pour boiling water over chilies to cover in bowl; let stand 10 to 15 minutes. Drain, reserving ³/₄ cup liquid.

2. Spray small skillet with cooking spray; heat over medium heat until hot. Add sesame seed and spices and cook over medium heat until seeds are toasted, 1 to 2 minutes, stirring constantly; remove from skillet. Add raisins, almonds, and pumpkin seed and cook over medium

heat until toasted, 1 to 2 minutes, stirring constantly; remove from skillet. Add onion and garlic to skillet; saute until tender, 2 to 3 minutes, and remove from skillet.

3. Spray tortilla lightly with cooking spray; cook in skillet over medium heat until browned, about 1 minute on each side. Cool tortilla; cut into 1-inch pieces.

4. Process chilies, onion mixture, and tomato in blender until smooth. Add sesame seed-spice mixture, raisin mixture, reserved chili liquid, and tortilla; process, adding enough chicken broth to make smooth, thick mixture.

5. Spray large skillet with cooking spray; heat over medium heat until hot. Add sauce; stir in cocoa and remaining chicken broth. Heat to boiling; reduce heat and simmer, uncovered, 5 minutes, stirring frequently. Season to taste with salt. Makes about 3 cups.

Nutritional Data

PER SERVING		EXCHANGES	
Calories:	57	Milk:	0.0
% Calories from fat:	30	Vegetable:	1.0
Fat (gm):	2.1	Fruit:	0.0
Sat. fat (gm):	0.3	Bread:	0.0
Cholesterol (mg):	0	Meat:	0.0
Sodium (gm):	20	Fat:	0.0
Protein (gm):	2.7		
Carbohydrate (gm):	8.4		

10
DESSERTS

Sugar and Rum Plantains

Caramel Flan

Pineapple Flan

Raisin Bread Pudding

Cinnamon Rice Pudding

Buñuelos

Sweet Tamales

Fruit Empanadas

SUGAR AND RUM PLANTAINS

◆

*Purchase ripe plantains that are soft
with blackened skins. Pineapple or orange juice
can be substituted for the rum, if desired.*

Serves 4

1 tablespoon margarine
2 ripe plantains, peeled, diagonally cut into
   ¼-inch slices
½ cup dark rum
⅓ cup sugar
4 tablespoons fat-free sour cream
   Ground cinnamon, to taste
1 tablespoon pine nuts, toasted

1. Melt margarine in large skillet; arrange plantains in skillet in single
layer. Cook over medium to medium-high heat until plantains are
browned, 2 to 3 minutes each side. Arrange on serving plates.

2. Add rum and sugar to skillet; heat to boiling. Reduce heat and simmer,
stirring constantly, until mixture is reduced to a thick glaze
consistency. Drizzle syrup over plantains; top each serving with a
dollop of sour cream. Sprinkle with cinnamon and nuts.

Nutritional Data

PER SERVING		EXCHANGES	
Calories:	284	Milk:	0.0
% Calories from fat:	13	Vegetable:	0.0
Fat (gm):	4.4	Fruit:	2.0
Sat. fat (gm):	0.7	Bread:	1.0
Cholesterol (mg):	0	Meat:	0.0
Sodium (gm):	46	Fat:	1.0
Protein (gm):	2.7		
Carbohydrate (gm):	47		

CARAMEL FLAN

---

*Undoubtedly Mexico's favorite dessert! The caramelized
sugar creates a delicious caramel sauce to be spooned over
each serving. The Orange Flan is a variation you'll want to
try also. Serve either flan with fresh fruit.*

Serves 8 (about ⅔ cup each)

⅓ cup plus ½ cup sugar, divided
4 cups skim milk
3 eggs
4 egg whites, or ½ cup cholesterol-free egg
   product
2 teaspoons vanilla

1. Heat ⅓ cup sugar in small skillet over medium-high heat until sugar
melts and turns golden, stirring occasionally (watch carefully, as sugar
can burn easily!). Quickly pour syrup into bottom of 2-quart soufflé
dish or casserole and tilt dish to coat bottom completely. Cool.

2. Heat milk and remaining ½ cup sugar until steaming and just
beginning to bubble at edges. Beat eggs and egg whites in medium
bowl; whisk in hot milk and vanilla. Pour mixture through strainer
into prepared dish.

3. Place dish in roasting pan on middle oven rack. Cover dish with
aluminum foil or lid. Pour 2 inches of hot water into roasting pan.
Bake at 350 degrees until custard is just set in the center and a sharp
knife inserted halfway between center and edge comes out clean,
about 60 minutes. Remove dish from roasting pan; cool on wire rack.
Refrigerate 8 hours or overnight.

3. To unfold, loosen edge of custard with sharp knife. Place rimmed
serving plate over dish and invert.

Orange Flan

Make recipe as above, substituting ½ cup orange juice concentrate for
½ cup of the milk.

Nutritional Data (Caramel Flan)

PER SERVING		EXCHANGES	
Calories:	164	Milk:	0.5
% Calories from fat:	12	Vegetable:	0.0
Fat (gm):	2.1	Fruit:	0.0
Sat. fat (gm):	0.7	Bread:	1.5
Cholesterol (mg):	81.9	Meat:	0.5
Sodium (gm):	114	Fat:	0.0
Protein (gm):	8.3		
Carbohydrate (gm):	27.60		

PINEAPPLE FLAN

Another wonderful flan variation. Serve with fresh pineapple chunks and garnish with dollops of whipped topping.

Serves 8 (about ²/₃ cup each)

2/3 cup sugar, divided
3 cups unsweetened pineapple juice
1 cup 2% milk
3 eggs
4 egg whites, or ¹/₂ cup cholesterol-free egg
product
Mint leaves, as garnish

1. Heat ¹/₃ cup sugar in small skillet over medium-high heat until sugar melts and turns golden, stirring occasionally (watch carefully, as sugar can burn easily!). Quickly pour syrup into bottom of 2-quart soufflé dish or casserole and tilt dish to coat bottom completely. Cool.

2. Heat pineapple juice, milk, and remaining ¹/₃ cup sugar until steaming and just beginning to bubble at the edges. Beat eggs and egg whites in medium bowl; whisk in hot juice mixture. Pour mixture through strainer into prepared dish.

3. Place dish in roasting pan on middle oven rack. Cover dish with aluminum foil or lid. Pour 2 inches of hot water into roasting pan. Bake at 350 degrees until custard is just set in the center and a sharp knife inserted halfway between center and edge comes out clean, about 60 minutes. Remove dish from roasting pan; cool on wire rack. Refrigerate 8 hours or overnight.

3. To unfold, loosen edge of custard with sharp knife. Place rimmed serving plate over dish and invert. Garnish with mint leaves.

Nutritional Data

PER SERVING		EXCHANGES	
Calories:	169	Milk:	0.0
% Calories from fat:	13	Vegetable:	0.0
Fat (gm):	2.5	Fruit:	1.0
Sat. fat (gm):	1	Bread:	1.0
Cholesterol (mg):	82.1	Meat:	0.5
Sodium (gm):	68	Fat:	0.0
Protein (gm):	5.5		
Carbohydrate (gm):	31.6		

RAISIN BREAD PUDDING

In Mexico the crusty, firm-textured rolls called bolillos are typically used to make this toothsome pudding.

Serves 8

2½ cups skim milk
3 tablespoons margarine, cut into pieces
2 eggs, lightly beaten
1 teaspoon vanilla
¾ cup packed light brown sugar
1 teaspoon ground cinnamon
½ teaspoon ground nutmeg
¼ teaspoon salt
6 cups cubed firm-textured, or day-old, bread
½ cup raisins
Ground nutmeg, as garnish

1. Heat milk and margarine in small saucepan over medium-high heat until margarine is melted. Beat milk mixture into eggs; mix in vanilla, sugar, spices, and salt. Pour mixture over bread in large bowl; add raisins and toss.

2. Spoon mixture into lightly greased 2-quart casserole; sprinkle generously with nutmeg. Place casserole in roasting pan on oven rack; add 1½ inches of hot water. Bake, uncovered, at 350 degrees until pudding is set and a sharp knife inserted near center comes out clean, about 45 minutes. Serve warm.

Nutritional Data

PER SERVING		EXCHANGES	
Calories:	252	Milk:	0.5
% Calories from fat:	23	Vegetable:	0.0
Fat (gm):	6.6	Fruit:	0.5
Sat. fat (gm):	1.5	Bread:	2.0
Cholesterol (mg):	55	Meat:	0.0
Sodium (gm):	296	Fat:	1.0
Protein (gm):	6.3		
Carbohydrate (gm):	42.6		

CINNAMON RICE PUDDING

A true comfort food in any country!

Serves 6 (about ⅔ cup each)

1 cup long-grain rice
  Water
1 cinnamon stick, broken into pieces
1 quart skim milk
1 cup sugar
2 egg yolks
4 egg whites, or ½ cup cholesterol-free egg
  product
1 teaspoon vanilla
  Salt, to taste
2 tablespoons toasted pine nuts, or almonds
  Ground nutmeg, as garnish

1. In medium saucepan, cook rice in water according to package directions, adding cinnamon pieces to water.

2. Add milk to cooked rice; heat to boiling. Reduce heat and simmer, covered, until mixture starts to thicken, 20 to 25 minutes, stirring occasionally. Add sugar, stirring until dissolved; discard cinnamon pieces.

3. Beat egg yolks and whites in small bowl; stir in about 1 cup of rice mixture. Stir egg and rice mixture back into saucepan. Cook over low heat, stirring constantly, 2 to 3 minutes. Stir in vanilla; season to taste with salt.

3. Spoon pudding into serving dishes; sprinkle each with pine nuts and add nutmeg as garnish. Serve warm, or refrigerate and serve chilled.

Nutritional Data

PER SERVING		EXCHANGES	
Calories:	351	Milk:	0.5
% Calories from fat:	10	Vegetable:	0.0
Fat (gm):	3.9	Fruit:	0.0
Sat. fat (gm):	0.8	Bread:	4.0
Cholesterol (mg):	73.7	Meat:	0.0
Sodium (gm):	125	Fat:	0.5
Protein (gm):	11.7		
Carbohydrate (gm):	67.5		

BUÑUELOS

*Although enjoyed year round in Mexico, these crisp
treats are a Christmas Eve tradition, often served
with mugs of steaming hot chocolate.*

Makes 36

2 cups all-purpose flour, divided
1 tablespoon sugar
½ teaspoon baking powder
¼ teaspoon salt
2 tablespoons margarine, cut into pieces
2 egg whites, lightly beaten
¼ cup skim milk
Vegetable oil
½ cup sugar
1–2 teaspoons ground cinnamon

1. Combine 1⅔ cups flour, 1 tablespoon sugar, baking powder, and salt in medium bowl; cut in margarine with pastry blender until mixture resembles coarse crumbs. Mix combined eggs and milk into flour mixture, adding remaining flour a tablespoon at a time to form a soft dough. Knead dough on lightly floured surface 2 to 3 minutes.

2. Shape dough into log; divide into 36 pieces. Roll each piece of dough on floured surface to form circle about 3 inches in diameter (dough will be paper thin). Let stand while rolling remaining dough.

3. Heat 2 inches of oil to 375 degrees in deep skillet. Fry buñuelos, a few at a time, until puffed and golden, about 30 seconds on each side. Drain well on paper toweling. Sprinkle with combined ½ cup sugar and cinnamon while warm. Makes 3 dozen.

Nutritional Data

PER BUÑUELO		EXCHANGES	
Calories:	42	Milk:	0.0
% Calories from fat:	18	Vegetable:	0.0
Fat (gm):	0.8	Fruit:	0.0
Sat. fat (gm):	0.2	Bread:	0.5
Cholesterol (mg):	0	Meat:	0.0
Sodium (gm):	31	Fat:	0.0
Protein (gm):	0.9		
Carbohydrate (gm):	7.7		

SWEET TAMALES

An authentic ending to a festive Mexican meal!
The tamales can be made 2 to 3 days in advance and
can be reheated conveniently in a microwave oven.

Serves 8 (1 tamale each)

     8 corn husks
        Hot water
   2/3 cup grits
   1/2 cup warm fat-free, reduced-sodium chicken
        broth
     2 tablespoons margarine, softened
   1/3 cup sugar
   3/4 teaspoon ground cinnamon
   1/4 teaspoon ground nutmeg
   1/4 teaspoon baking powder
   1/4 teaspoon salt
   1/4 cup chopped dried apple
   1/4 cup chopped candied fruit, or raisins
     2 tablespoons chopped almonds, or pine nuts

1. Soak corn husks in hot water until softened, about 1 hour; drain well on paper toweling.

2. Process grits in blender (not a food processor!) until finely ground. Add chicken broth, margarine, sugar, spices, baking powder, and salt to blender; process until smooth. Process at high speed for 2 minutes. Mix in apple, candied fruit, and almonds.

3. Spread grits mixture in centers of corn husks, to within 2 inches of ends. Fold sides of each husk over filling; fold top and bottom of husk toward center and tie with string.

4. Place tamales on steamer rack in saucepan with 2 inches of water. Steam, covered, 2 hours, adding more water to saucepan if necessary. Serve warm or at room temperature.

Nutritional Data

PER SERVING		EXCHANGES	
Calories:	142	Milk:	0.0
% Calories from fat:	25	Vegetable:	0.0
Fat (gm):	4	Fruit:	0.0
Sat. fat (gm):	0.7	Bread:	1.5
Cholesterol (mg):	0	Meat:	0.0
Sodium (gm):	117	Fat:	0.5
Protein (gm):	1.9		
Carbohydrate (gm):	25.3		

FRUIT EMPANADAS

◆

Sweet empanadas can be served as an appetizer or dessert. Other dried fruits, such as pears or apples, can be substituted for the apricots and raisins.

Makes 24

½ cup chopped dried apricots
½ cup raisins
½ cup water
¼ cup sugar
½ teaspoon ground cinnamon
⅛ teaspoon ground nutmeg
  Empanada Pastry (see p. 15)
3 tablespoons skim milk, for glaze
1 tablespoon sugar, for glaze

1. Heat apricots, raisins, and water to boiling in small saucepan. Reduce heat and simmer, covered, until fruit is very soft, about 5 minutes. Mash fruit with fork until almost smooth; stir in ¼ cup sugar and spices.

2. Roll half the Empanada Pastry on lightly floured surface until ⅛ inch thick; cut into circles with 3-inch cookie cutter. Place slightly rounded teaspoon of fruit mixture in center of each pastry circle; fold pastries in half and crimp edges with tines of fork. Make slit in top of each pastry with knife.

3. Bake pastries on greased jellyroll pans at 350 degrees until golden, 12 to 15 minutes.

4. To glaze, brush pastries lightly with skim milk and sprinkle with sugar; bake 1 to 2 minutes more, until glazed. Serve warm. Makes about 2 dozen.

Nutritional Data

PER EMPANADA		EXCHANGES	
Calories:	64	Milk:	0.0
% Calories from fat:	23	Vegetable:	0.0
Fat (gm):	1.7	Fruit:	1.0
Sat. fat (gm):	0.4	Bread:	0.0
Cholesterol (mg):	0	Meat:	0.0
Sodium (gm):	16	Fat:	0.0
Protein (gm):	1		
Carbohydrate (gm):	11.8		

11
BEVERAGES

Margaritas

Sangria

Eggnog with Rum

Sweet Cinnamon Coffee

Tropical Fruit Shake

MARGARITAS

◆

Mexico's favorite libation! For best flavor, use fresh lime juice.

Serves 2 (about 4 ozs. each)

1 lime wedge
Coarse salt (optional)
½ cup tequila
¼ cup fresh lime juice
2 tablespoons orange liqueur
Ice

1. Rub rims of 2 margarita, or stemmed, glasses with lime wedge; dip rims in salt.

2. Mix tequila, lime juice, and orange liqueur. Serve over ice in glasses.

Nutritional Data

PER SERVING		EXCHANGES	
Calories:	185	Milk:	0.0
% Calories from fat:	0	Vegetable:	0.0
Fat (gm):	0	Fruit:	0.5
Sat. fat (gm):	0	Bread:	0.0
Cholesterol (mg):	0	Meat:	0.0
Sodium (gm):	1	Fat:	3.5
Protein (gm):	0.2		
Carbohydrate (gm):	8.6		

Strawberry Margaritas

In Step 2, process tequila, lime juice, orange liqueur, and 12 to 14 fresh or frozen strawberries in food processor or blender until smooth. Serve over ice in margarita, or stemmed, glasses.

SANGRIA

Mexico has adapted this famous Spanish wine punch; it also can be made with the addition of sparkling water. Serve well chilled.

Serves 12 (about ½ cup each)

- 4 cups dry red wine, chilled
- 2 cups orange juice, chilled
- ¼ cup lime juice
- ¾–1 cup sugar
- ½ lime, thinly sliced
- ½ orange, thinly sliced
- Ice

1. Mix wine, juices, and sugar in large pitcher, stirring until sugar is dissolved. Add fruit slices to pitcher; serve over ice in tall glasses.

Nutritional Data

PER SERVING		EXCHANGES	
Calories:	125	Milk:	0.0
% Calories from fat:	0.5	Vegetable:	0.0
Fat (gm):	0.1	Fruit:	0.5
Sat. fat (gm):	0	Bread:	0.5
Cholesterol (mg):	0	Meat:	0.0
Sodium (gm):	51	Fat:	1.2
Protein (gm):	0.6		
Carbohydrate (gm):	18.7		

EGGNOG WITH RUM

A holiday favorite—thick, rich, and creamy!

Serves 12 (about ½ cup each)

½ cup sugar
2 tablespoons cornstarch
1 quart skim milk, divided
2 eggs, beaten
1–1½ cups light rum
1 cup light whipped topping
Ground cinnamon, or nutmeg, as garnish

1. Mix sugar, cornstarch, and 3 cups milk in medium saucepan; heat to boiling, stirring frequently. Boil, stirring constantly, until thickened, about 1 minute.

2. Stir about half the milk mixture into the eggs; stir egg mixture back into saucepan. Cook over low heat, stirring constantly, 1 minute longer. Cool; refrigerate until chilled, 3 to 4 hours.

3. Stir remaining 1 cup milk and rum into eggnog; stir in whipped topping. Serve eggnog in small glasses or mugs; sprinkle with cinnamon.

Nutritional Data

PER SERVING		EXCHANGES	
Calories:	133	Milk:	0.5
% Calories from fat:	12	Vegetable:	0.0
Fat (gm):	1.7	Fruit:	0.0
Sat. fat (gm):	0.4	Bread:	0.5
Cholesterol (mg):	37	Meat:	0.0
Sodium (gm):	57	Fat:	1.5
Protein (gm):	3.8		
Carbohydrate (gm):	15		

SWEET CINNAMON COFFEE

◆

Serve hot, or chill and serve over ice.

Serves 8 (about 1/2 cup each)

4 cups water
1/3–1/2 cup packed brown sugar
1 small cinnamon stick
4 whole cloves
1/4 cup dark roast, regular-grind coffee

1. Heat water, brown sugar, and spices to boiling in medium saucepan; stir in coffee. Reduce heat and simmer, covered, 2 to 3 minutes. Remove from heat and let stand 2 to 3 minutes for grounds to settle.
2. Strain coffee; serve in small mugs.

Nutritional Data

PER SERVING		EXCHANGES	
Calories:	37	Milk:	0.0
% Calories from fat:	0	Vegetable:	0.0
Fat (gm):	0	Fruit:	0.0
Sat. fat (gm):	0	Bread:	0.5
Cholesterol (mg):	0	Meat:	0.0
Sodium (gm):	6	Fat:	0.0
Protein (gm):	0.1		
Carbohydrate (gm):	9.4		

TROPICAL FRUIT SHAKE

Fruit shakes, or licuados, are popular throughout Mexico and South America. Use any ripe fruit and vary flavors with honey, lemon juice, or native rum!

Serves 4 (about 1 cup each)

3 cups cubed pineapple, banana, melon, strawberries, or other ripe fruit
1 cup fat-free frozen vanilla yogurt
½ cup skim milk, chilled
3–4 tablespoons honey
  Ice cubes
  Nutmeg, freshly grated, as garnish

1. Process fruit, yogurt, milk, and honey in blender until smooth. Pour over ice in tall glasses; sprinkle with nutmeg.

Nutritional Data

PER SERVING		EXCHANGES	
Calories:	172	Milk:	0.0
% Calories from fat:	3	Vegetable:	0.0
Fat (gm):	0.6	Fruit:	2.0
Sat. fat (gm):	0.1	Bread:	0.5
Cholesterol (mg):	0.5	Meat:	0.0
Sodium (gm):	45	Fat:	0.0
Protein (gm):	3		
Carbohydrate (gm):	40.6		

12
BREADS

Bolillos

"Little Pants" Biscuits

Three Kings Bread

Green Chili Cornbread

BOLILLOS

◆

Bolillos are the crusty, "bobbin-shaped" yeast rolls that
are popular throughout Mexico. The dough is similar
to French bread dough.

Makes 12 rolls

   1 package active dry yeast
  ½ teaspoon sugar
   1 cup hot water (110–115 degrees)
   2 tablespoons vegetable shortening, room
     temperature
3½–4 cups all-purpose flour
  ½ teaspoon salt
   2 tablespoons skim milk

1. Mix yeast, sugar, and hot water in medium mixing bowl; add shortening, stirring until melted. Let stand 5 minutes.

2. Mix in 3½ cups of flour and the salt; mix in enough remaining flour to make soft dough. Knead dough on floured surface until smooth and elastic, about 5 minutes. Place dough in greased bowl; let stand, covered, in a warm place until dough is double in size, 1 to 1½ hours. Punch dough down.

3. Divide dough into 12 equal pieces. Roll or pat 1 piece of dough into an oval shape, a scant ½ inch thick. Fold ⅓ of the dough (long edge) toward the center and flatten with palm of hand; fold dough in half and flatten with palm of hand. Roll dough lightly with hand to make a rounded oval shape; place, seam side up, on lightly greased cookie sheet. Repeat with remaining dough. Let rolls stand, loosely covered, until double in size, about 1 hour.

4. Brush tops of bolillos lightly with milk. Bake at 375 degrees until lightly browned, about 25 minutes.

Nutritional Data

PER ROLL

		EXCHANGES	
Calories:	155	Milk:	0.0
% Calories from fat:	15	Vegetable:	0.0
Fat (gm):	2.5	Fruit:	0.0
Sat. fat (gm):	0.6	Bread:	2.0
Cholesterol (mg):	0	Meat:	0.0
Sodium (gm):	91	Fat:	0.5
Protein (gm):	4.1		
Carbohydrate (gm):	28.4		

"LITTLE PANTS" BISCUITS

*These sugar- and cinnamon-topped breads are sort
of a cross between a biscuit and a cookie. They are usually
made into "pants" shapes but can be cut into rounds or
squares if you prefer.*

Makes 18 biscuits

4 tablespoons vegetable shortening
½ cup sugar, divided
2 cups all-purpose flour
2 teaspoons baking powder
½ teaspoon salt
½ cup plus 2 tablespoons skim milk, divided
½ teaspoon ground cinnamon

1. Beat shortening and 6 tablespoons sugar in medium bowl until smooth. Beat in combined flour, baking powder, and salt, alternately with ½ cup milk to form soft dough.

2. Roll dough on floured surface into a rectangle, a scant ½ inch thick. Cut dough into trapezoid shapes, 2½ inches long on the bottom, 1½ inches on the top, and 3 inches on the sides. Cut out a small wedge of dough from the bottom, center of each piece to form "pants legs."

3. Lightly brush biscuits with remaining 2 tablespoons of milk. Mix the remaining 2 tablespoons of sugar with the cinnamon; sprinkle over biscuits.

4. Bake at 350 degrees on lightly greased cookie sheet until browned, 15 to 20 minutes. Serve warm.

Nutritional Data

PER BISCUIT		EXCHANGES	
Calories:	101	Milk:	0.0
% Calories from fat:	27	Vegetable:	0.0
Fat (gm):	3	Fruit:	0.0
Sat. fat (gm):	0.8	Bread:	1.0
Cholesterol (mg):	0.1	Meat:	0.0
Sodium (gm):	100	Fat:	0.5
Protein (gm):	1.7		
Carbohydrate (gm):	16.7		

THREE KINGS BREAD

◆

This rich fruit-studded bread is traditionally served to celebrate Twelfth Night on January 6. A tiny china doll is often baked into the dough; the person receiving the piece of bread with the doll must give a party on February 2 to celebrate the Feast of the Candles! As china dolls are difficult to find, we've given directions for using a small plastic doll.

Serves 12 (1 loaf)

1 package active dry yeast
1/3 cup very warm skim milk (110–115 degrees)
2 1/4–2 3/4 cups all-purpose flour, divided
6 tablespoons margarine, softened
1/4 cup plus 2 tablespoons sugar, divided
1 egg
2 egg whites
1/2 teaspoon salt
1/4 cup dark raisins
1/2 cup candied fruit, divided
1/4 cup chopped walnuts (optional)
1–2 tablespoons skim milk

1. Mix yeast, warm milk, and 1/2 cup flour in small bowl; beat well. Let stand, covered, in a warm place for 30 minutes.

2. Beat margarine and 1/4 cup sugar in medium bowl until fluffy. Beat in egg, egg whites, and salt. Add yeast mixture, mixing well. Mix in raisins, 1/4 cup candied fruit, walnuts (optional), and enough of the remaining 1 3/4 cups flour to make soft dough. Knead on floured surface until smooth and elastic, about 5 minutes. Place dough in greased bowl; let stand, covered, in a warm place until dough is double in size, about 1 hour. Punch dough down.

3. Form dough into a round on greased cookie sheet. Make a hole in center of dough, then stretch with fingers into a ring 8 inches in diameter. Let rise, covered, in a warm place until double in size, about 30 minutes. Decorate with remaining 1/4 cup of candied fruit.

4. Bake at 375 degrees until bread is golden, 25 to 30 minutes. Brush bread with 1 to 2 tablespoons of milk and sprinkle with remaining 2 tablespoons of sugar. Bake until glazed, 3 to 5 minutes longer. Cool on wire rack.

5. Remove from oven and turn bread upside down. To follow tradition, cut out a small wedge of bread from anywhere in the loaf, and insert a tiny plastic doll; replace wedge.

Nutritional Data

PER SERVING		EXCHANGES	
Calories:	205	Milk:	0.0
% Calories from fat:	28	Vegetable:	0.0
Fat (gm):	6.3	Fruit:	0.5
Sat. fat (gm):	1.3	Bread:	1.5
Cholesterol (mg):	17.9	Meat:	0.0
Sodium (gm):	174	Fat:	1.5
Protein (gm):	4.2		
Carbohydrate (gm):	33.1		

GREEN CHILI CORNBREAD

*If using mild canned chilies, consider adding a teaspoon or
so of minced jalapeño chili for a piquant accent. Serve this
flavorful cornbread warm.*

Serves 9

Vegetable cooking spray
1/4 cup chopped red bell pepper
2 cloves garlic, minced
1/2 teaspoon cumin seed, crushed
1¼ cups yellow cornmeal
3/4 cup all-purpose flour
2 teaspoons baking powder
1/2 teaspoon baking soda
1 teaspoon sugar
1/2 teaspoon salt
1¼ cups buttermilk
1/2 cup canned cream-style corn
1 can (4 ounces) chopped hot or mild green
chilies, well drained
1 egg
2 egg whites
3½ tablespoons margarine, melted

1. Spray small skillet with cooking spray; heat over medium heat until hot. Saute red bell pepper, garlic, and cumin seed until pepper is tender, 2 to 3 minutes.

2. Combine cornmeal, flour, baking powder, baking soda, sugar, and salt in large bowl. Add buttermilk, bell pepper mixture and remaining ingredients; mix until smooth. Spread batter in greased 8-inch-square baking pan.

3. Bake at 425 degrees until cornbread is golden, about 30 minutes. Cool in pan on wire rack.

Nutritional Data

PER SERVING

Calories:	184			
% Calories from fat:	29			
Fat (gm):	6.1			
Sat. fat (gm):	1.3			
Cholesterol (mg):	24.9			
Sodium (gm):	562			
Protein (gm):	5.6			
Carbohydrate (gm):	27.6			

EXCHANGES

Milk:	0.0
Vegetable:	0.0
Fruit:	0.0
Bread:	2.0
Meat:	0.0
Fat:	1.0

INDEX